The Only Road That Leads Home

By Cheryl A. Hardy

The Only Road That Leads Home
Copyright 2015 by Cheryl A. Hardy

All rights reserved. No part of this book may be reproduced or copied in any form without written permission from Cheryl A. Hardy.

ISBN-13:978-1516864065
ISBN-10:1516864069
Printed by CreateSpace, an Amazon.com Company

Scripture quotations marked HCSB have been taken from the Holman Christian Standard Bible, Copyright 1999, 2000, 2002, 2003, 2009 by Holman Bible Publishers. Used by permission. Holman Christian Standard Bible, Holman CSB, and HCSB are federally registered trademarks of Holman Bible Publishers.

Dedication

To my Lord and Savior, my grandparents, parents, my soul mate and husband- Richard, our four "perfect" children- Robin, Dustin, Landin, and Kalin, and our seven wonderful grandchildren. Many "thank yous" were heartfelt as I sat down and began to let the words flow for this effort to record a bit of family history. I am most appreciative to my Lord that has blessed this family throughout the years. Had God not been a part, this family as I have known it, would not exist. God's love has served as the very foundation for this family to build upon. I am thankful to Grandmother and Grandaddy, and their parents before them, for weaving the very fibers of family love and Christian values into our history and giving me the opportunity to observe sacrifice, sincerity, unabashed care, and devotion to family and to community. Many thanks go to Mother and Daddy for making God and family a deliberate priority for us. I realize as an adult my life could have turned out much differently if their priorities were placed elsewhere. I am deeply grateful for Richard- for his example in being a Christian father, his patience, hard work, unending love, and consistency in our own family. I can truly call him my better half and I love him so very much! Then there are our four "perfect wonders" that we call our children. Every time that we had another baby, I saw a phenomenal love increase without measure. Thank you Robin, Dustin, Landin, and Kalin for making our lives full of fun, laughter, love...and lots of hard work! And now, with seven little grandsons, our life has even more room for love, snuggles, and giggles! How very thankful I am for Caden, Grant, Reese, Jake, Caleb, Merritt, and Jaxon! Who knew a person could have so much!

Introduction

"Richly blessed" is the phrase I use to summarize the years. My intent in sharing this manuscript is to prove that point. Not long ago I drove Uncle Charles and Aunt June to the funeral of their grandson, Michael. While we visited going and coming the entire day, we kept coming back to the years that we lived across the road from each other- the years that I was under their feet, and the memories we both shared. It was truly a wonderful visit despite the curtain of sadness looming over the day. As we approached the black-top road that turned off of Hwy 59 on the way back home, Uncle Charles leaned forward in the car and stated, "Now we turn right up here. It's crooked,...but it's the only road that leads home." His statement resounded across my thoughts. It hung in the air and continued to echo in the days afterward. How very true, not only about the narrow road, but also about life. As you read the following recollections through the years, you will see the memories form a crooked road into the fiber of my life. But then again,...it's the only road that leads home.

Chapters

1. Fig Newtons in Our Bed
2. Childhood Security
3. Failure to Launch
4. Children and Diabetes
5. The Circle M
6. A Child's Christmas
7. Other Holidays
8. Sharing a Bedroom
9. Raising Chickens in Texas
10. Life on the Circle M
11. Grandaddy's Beans
12. Mother and Daddy's Hobbies
13. We were Poor
14. Working Alongside
15. Company
16. Birthdays
17. Toys
18. Signs of the Times
19. Doctors and Dentists
20. Vacations
21. Discipline
22. Chores
23. Not an Only Child
24. Our Social Fun
25. Cousins
26. The Shamrock
27. The Influence of Church
28. Early School Days
29. Don't Buy Me Any Furniture
30. Jr. High and High School
31. Daddy's Planes
32. Mother and Daddy's 25th Anniversary
33. Dating
34. Wedding Bells
35. Poor, Barefoot, but Not Pregnant
36. Time to Teach
37. The Big Pool and Daddy's Heart Attack
38. Harleton Culture Shock
39. Babies
40. Anniversaries
41. Raise the Bar
42. From This Point Forward

Here are a few glimpses into my past. My thoughts have roamed freely as the cobwebs within my brain have retraced and recalled memories and events from "back when." May you chuckle occasionally, share in the moments of sadness, grow in your understanding of our family, and smile in contentment as you realize so many similar aspects have simply been passed on for your family to ...enjoy, endure, and endear. As that realization *really* hits home, just understand there is nothing you can do about it. This is family. This is life.

1. Fig Newtons in Our Bed

My earliest memory as a child was at age two. My great grandmother Johnson was living in the back bedroom at Grandmother Hancock's house. She was bedridden- but loved for me to visit with her. She would get a sparkle in her eye and ask me to sneak into the kitchen and get us some fig newton's from the cookie jar. Of course, as a two year old, it never dawned on me that when I got to the kitchen and asked for help to get into the cookie jar, that the adults knew exactly what was going on. I would return to the bedroom with a fist full of newtons, and climb up on the bed, and like two queens on our throne, guarding the utmost secret, we would eat cookies in bed. That was an absolute "no-no" in my grandmother's and my own house as well. She and I would giggle like we had some great treasure that no other person in the house knew about, and all along they not only knew, but played along with the game that was orchestrated by a sweet elderly great-grandmother that doted over the youngster in her room.

That is my only memory of Great-grandmother. She died a short time later. Mother tells that Grandmother Hancock almost worked herself to death taking care of her in her last days- there was no hospice, and no other sibling that took turns in her care- just Grandmother. The entire family considered Grandmother Hancock a rock- nothing came along that she could not handle.

2. Childhood Security

I guess the sense of security was deeply engrained into my childhood from the very beginning. I always felt Mother and Daddy could handle any situation, relieve any fear, tackle any problem. I was completely at home in our house at the Circle M. That security and sense of being loved without question was reinforced through Grandmother and Grandaddy. Their house was as much home as anywhere I have ever lived. I think I saw Mother and Daddy consider Grandmother and Grandaddy's as their security and safe haven, and it made me double-blessed. I can describe the place as it was when I was a child, and there is a sense of peace that floods my soul to this day.

We were always welcome at Grandmother and Grandaddy's. We never called and asked to come to lunch, we just showed up and somehow she always had more than enough- always fresh from the garden. The trips to the garden were always done before 9:00 AM so she still had time to wash the greens, shell the peas, scrub the new potatoes, and make sure the meat was done before lunch. She rolled her dumplings with a whiskey bottle- one of only two that ever were in the house. The second was also in the kitchen, kept behind other things in the top right cabinet. It contained the whiskey used only for cutting cough and croup. Every meal began with either homemade biscuits-starting with the flour bowl and making a "well" in the flour followed by an "egg" of grease- or the meal began with a pan of homemade cornbread. She had a neat little pan with an attached metal slide that loosened the cornbread when it was cooked. These lunches were my first memory of true contentment. It is also my first memory of Grandmother's gingerbread. She would pop a pan in the oven as we sat down to eat, and it would come out smelling like cinnamon and nutmeg just about the time we completed our meal. That smell still makes me think of Grandmother to this day. Supper was always cornbread and milk in a cold metal glass and leftovers from lunch. Since the grand kids hadn't taken such a liking to that being supper, Grandmother always kept cans of Campbell's Chicken Noodle for the times we were sharing supper.

Summer birthdays or anniversaries were celebrated with pound cake- I never remember a cake at their house with icing- and homemade ice cream. Granddaddy's favorite was strawberry. Of course, Grandaddy always kept mellorine in the back porch freezer- Neapolitan. I would always try to get the chocolate first, hoping I could avoid the strawberry as it was my least favorite.

Winter meals sometimes consisted of a pot of homemade soup- but mostly the vegetables and meats she had canned during the summer. We shelled many peas and beans under the China berry tree, climbed the pecan trees over the lawnmower shed, and played hide-n-seek in the smokehouse, outhouse, cellar, and sweet potato house that all flanked the back yard. Late afternoons brought trips to the barn to milk and gather the eggs, to turn the cows and calves out, and check on whatever other animals they had at the time. Grandaddy always had the philosophy that he wouldn't feed an animal that didn't have a job. He never kept a dog. That was feeding a useless animal. The occasional cat stayed at the barn and earned its keep by killing mice and chicken snakes.

The clickety-clack of the windmill blades turning by

the well in the back yard, and the sound of kids hitting the metal cistern outside the back porch as we ran around the house playing chase were comfort sounds. Close to the back walk and to the side were flowerbeds- her climbing roses climbed to the eaves of the house and the back porch was always filled with their fragrance during the summer, I remember specifically a white rose tinged in pink, a large red rose, and a prolific yellow one, too. Grandmother loved them, and they frequented her kitchen window often.

Spring brought all the jonquils and daffodils to bloom and our little fingers couldn't resist bringing at least one stubby, stinky fistful into the house to put in a colored metal glass on the table. Then there were pink wild roses up the fence on both sides of the road by the store that we made a point to visit in early May as well.

I miss the house that Grandmother and Grandaddy lived in. It was always inviting with its green siding and concrete walk leading to the front porch flanked by red-orange brick banisters and Nandinas on either side. I can still place each piece of furniture there, smell the shrubbery outside the front bedroom window, and dredge up so many memories from within its walls. I can see the apple cookie jar on the counter top hoarding its stash of banana taffy, lemon drops and fig newtons. I can almost hear the conversations around the red Formica table as we savored the meal that Grandmother had lovingly prepared without "knowing that we would be there." Boisterous Christmas dinners for the entire family spread food and laughter completely throughout the house as we found places to sit and eat the feast of the day. While grownups claimed the dining room for seating, the food lined tables that stretched through the French doors, covered the buffet, the adult table, and the kitchen stove! And in contrast, I treasured the times we visited simply, in their bedrooms around the heater with the both of them sitting and rocking "ever so easy" in their rockers.

Oh, and the back porch was the "room of versatility." From a nap on the red divan, to clothes hung inside on the line by the screen walls, to eating at the little red counter surrounding the well; it was able to accommodate any task. At times there were spread newspapers covered with ripening tomatoes, bushels of peas waiting on shelling, followed by newspapers spread with watermelon seed or unshelled beans/peas drying so Grandaddy could save the seed. There might be a couple of watermelons waiting to be cut. Then there was always a place just to sit down and cool off with a glass of cool water in one of the cane-bottomed chairs against the wall. The back porch also held the freezer. This wasn't a typical freezer- it had three full size doors. It was somewhere between 9 and 12 foot long and we all knew where the mellorine was stashed, as was Grandaddy's jars of seed for next year. It also housed the hundreds of packages or plastic freezer cartons of fruits and vegetables that noted the countless hours of work Grandmother had given in preparation for winter.

The living room was immaculate at all times. Grandmother kept her pictures of the grand-kids on a writing table there, and her writing supplies and loose pictures in the drawer underneath. The marble mantle was home to the black wind up mantle clock that never kept accurate time in my lifetime, but balanced the mantle nonetheless. The marble hearth below provided cold extra seating when the room filled with family during holidays. Some of the little things I see to this day- the glass ash trays, the doilies on the back of the couch and on the arms of the chair in my very young days, the flower encrusted candy dish on the coffee table, the bookcase flanking the corner, the telephone table hovering near the front door, Grandmother's rocker by the hallway, and Grandaddy's in front of the TV holding the red shade lamp from Okinawa still grace the memory of that wonderful room. I loved the living room linoleum that looked like short-looped carpet under glass, the tall ceiling, and the gas logs in the fireplace. The glass doors leading into the dining room along with the built-in display cabinet were intriguing to me. It seemed that her French doors were the one place that Grandmother convinced Grandaddy to splurge when building the house.

The outside was just as enticing to a youngster seeking places to play. Out front was a huge oak. Hedge made a fence across the front, and was divided into two sections by a metal gate and concrete sidewalk leading up to the front porch. On either side of the walk were two round concrete-edged flowerbeds that heralded spring with the most majestic hyacinths I've ever seen. I watched Grandaddy bring a wheelbarrow of chicken house manure every fall and spread, under Grandmother's orders, an even 2 inch layer over the dormant beds. In spring, the hyacinths would come up through the manure, making 10-12 in spikes loaded with the most fragrant hyacinths this side of Heaven.

Along the road on the left, was Grandaddy's store. It stayed open until I was around 6 years old. If someone wanted to buy something, they would go to the house and get someone there to come open it up for the purchase. He carried everything from nails and hardware to Cokes, sewing thread, and Black Drought. I have eavesdropped on many conversations there from hired hands to the neighbors down the road. I've watched many come buy a slice of cheese, a sleeve of crackers, a "sodie" water, and a bear claw for lunch. Sometimes they might add a can of viennas or drink a RC. Staples in the food line were always present, and it was the place a kid definitely wanted to hang out for conversations alone. My favorite part of the store was the candy counter. It was there that my bare foot would allow my big toe to find the rat hole chewed into the wood near the bottom. Around and around it would move until I could make the decision as to which candy bar I would choose that time, and it was always a Zero bar!

    Behind the store, running alongside the left of the house and just outside the yard fence was a row of pecan trees. These were the little native pecans, wonderful in flavor, but not very large. It was these that Grandmother picked out for her pecan pies. At the back left inside the yard was the lawnmower/oil shed. It smelled like oil and diesel, but we learned how to shimmy up the side to get into the largest pecan tree sitting right beside that shed. Along the back fence of the yard was the potato shed where Grandaddy stored his sweet potatoes in bushel baskets throughout the winter. When we were bored or hungry, we would go get a knife from the kitchen along with some sugar, come back and slice up a raw sweet potato, sprinkle it with sugar, and eat it for snack. I'm told that we don't digest raw sweet potatoes, but it didn't stop us, and none of us were ever sick with a stomach ache. Flowerbeds filled with hollyhocks, poppies, and gladiolas ran along the back fence in the right back corner. She filled in with other things, but these were the flowers I remember her adding to the bouquets she prepared for church each week during blooming season. On the right back sat the outhouse. It was a two-holer, and was available until I was an early teen. Along the fence sat the household chicken coop for Grandaddy's and Grandmother's laying hens. This was part of a large multipurpose building, which included storage and a porch- complete with hanging scales. It was here that if someone came to purchase a chicken or two, they were weighed so Grandaddy knew how much to charge them. It was also here that Grandmother stashed her hoe and rake and a couple of yard brooms. On the back side of this building was the smokehouse. Inside it was a saltbox where the hams were salted down, and the stuffed sausages rode the rafters. Also along the right hand fence was a china berry tree beside a filled in goldfish pond that belonged to my mother. The China berry tree was the location of many summer afternoon conversations as we shucked corn, shelled purple-hull, cream, and crowder peas, along with butter beans, pintos, and limas. There was always work to be done, but the work was always done in stride. It was just part of the day, and while we were trailing behind Grandmother and Grandaddy or Mother and Daddy, we knew we belonged. Whether we were working or playing, we never tired of being at Grandmother and Grandaddy's.

3. Failure to Launch

I was told that my mother and daddy's courtship was a whirlwind. They started dating in the May of 1956 and married August 8, 1956. When Daddy came to pick up Mother to get married, they simply told Grandmother and Grandaddy they were going to the preacher's house to get married. Mother's cousin, Norma and her date, Aaron Bean, served as Maid of Honor and Best Man. I always wondered what Grandmother and Grandaddy thought following the announcement, or if they were disappointed by not being invited to witness the wedding. Nevertheless, it was as simple as it could be made, and the marriage a community said would never work, began. Daddy was working for Coca-Cola in Center so they got an upstairs apartment just off the square in Center for the first six months they were married. Mother had always been raised in the country, and had never been exposed to the confines of the city. She absolutely hated it. There were no pastures to bush-hog, no chickens to feed, no horses to ride or brush, and no fields or woods to walk. She felt cooped up, and I am sure, daily let Daddy know it. After six months, he consented to moving back into Grandmother and Grandaddy Hancock's back bedroom. Most would have called this "failure to launch." In reality, it was the beginning of two different gears learning to connect the cogs of the wheels to move forward together. They lived there for about five years, until I was two. It was there that they learned the give and take of a marriage, bought their first furniture, had their first baby, bought their first car, had their first dog, and Daddy found the Lord.

4. Children and Diabetes

Mother was a juvenile diabetic. When she was six years old she had scarlet fever and it settled in her pancreas. No one knew it at the time; she just continued to lose weight. Grandmother was overworked, and Aunt Rosa Lee had recently married. She volunteered to let Mother stay with her during part of the summer. Mother became weak and when she brought her back home it wasn't long before Mother slipped into a coma. She wound up in Shreveport at Willis Knighten hospital. No one could diagnose or figure out what was going on. As God had planned it, the top diabetic doctor in the country from Chicago was visiting the hospital in Shreveport, as he was on his way to a conference in New Orleans, and had stopped by. Baffled, the doctors asked him to check on Mother. He walked into the room, and said, "She has diabetes. Give her a shot of insulin." Within an hour, mother was alert again. The doctor went on to explain that he smelled over-ripe bananas when he walked into her room- a dead give-away to the ketones being produced as muscle breaks down in a diabetic. She was diagnosed with diabetes in 1939. Insulin had been invented in 1933. Mother was six years old.

One of the drawbacks for the adult diabetic patient during the 1950's was trying to have children. Mother and Daddy had heard those warnings. There was only a one in three chance of being able to get pregnant, and then a one in three chance that she could carry until full term. Then there was only a one in three chance that she would deliver a live baby. That makes my arrival pretty incredible, one in 27 odds, especially with the additional problem of a lung that did not respond. Grandmother was praying the whole time, and began sewing little diaper shirts and cotton dresses with tiny smocking on the front. Daddy bought me a red dress with little red rubber pants to go underneath. Faith in action, as they believed in God's provision of a family.

There had been a new doctor move to Carthage, Dr. Grundy Cooper, and he was not discouraged by the statistics. He knew Mother was active and healthy, and he monitored her closely. By the end of the pregnancy, it looked like Mother might just deliver a baby after all. A nurse had already been assigned to sit by my incubator at birth since my pancreas had taken over the job of mine and Mother's during the pregnancy, alleviating the need for Mother to take insulin during the majority of that time. Doctors predicted that I would go through a diabetic reaction shortly after birth as my body adjusted to producing just enough insulin for my own small body instead of for Mother and me. Fortunately, on the Sunday Mother went into labor, she had already worked that morning in the chicken houses carrying 50 pound sacks of feed to the feeders from the feed room. Mother was physically in great shape, and was handling things really well, especially to be 8 ½ months along. Around lunch, Grandmother had gathered that things were changing and encouraged Mother and Daddy to go to the hospital (Panola General in Carthage, TX). I was born at 5:30 that afternoon and was home three days later- the picture of a normal delivery and hospital stay in the 1950's, and although one lung did not respond immediately, it did later that night. Shortly thereafter it was discovered, however, that Mother had undergone premature menopause immediately after my birth and could not have any further biological children. Since Mother and Daddy wanted a large family, one door closing simply guided them to find another door that was open, and Susan, John, Joyce, and Alan were God's intentional additions to the family through adoption.

Parenting was not without its trials, however. At two months I was threatened with my first spanking. Daddy was tired, and I was screaming in the middle of the night. Mother didn't know what to do to stop me from crying. Fortunately Grandmother heard me crying, came to my rescue, and took me to the back porch to rock me in the red rocker there. She laid my head against her chest and her hand over my other ear. Almost immediately I stopped crying. She reported back to Mother and Daddy that I had an earache, continued to rock me the rest of the night, and the next morning I was in the doctor's office getting antibiotics.

Mother was fully aware that being a diabetic had its challenges. Looking back, Grandaddy or Grandmother always popped in between 8:00 and 9:00AM every morning after Mother and Daddy built their house and moved out. I just thought it was family checking on each other, and realistically, it was that and more. Mother had taught me to call the operator before I was three years old. She would sit the phone in her lap; make me dial 0 while holding down the button on our black rotary dial phone so I actually would not make the call. She and I would rehearse what to say if Mother "was sick" and couldn't wake up. I knew to get her a Coke and peanut butter sandwich if she began to act "funny" and Daddy had prompted me in making Susan cry. Mother would be persuaded to do anything so her babies wouldn't cry when she was in a diabetic reaction, and Susan cried easier than I did. We could talk Mother into eating when the reaction was making her defiant if Susan was crying. Then we would distract Susan and she would stop. Mother had lots of reactions when she was a younger mother, but they leveled out as she got older and became progressively fewer in number. I'd like to think she gained more control of her diabetes, and in many ways she did limit what she ate, switched to Diet Dr. Pepper rather than real Coke, and learned to adjust her insulin in relation to the meals she had eaten. It was the diabetes that ultimately cut her life short, however at 53. It is truly a nasty disease.

  I was told by Margaret King from King's Nursery in Tenaha this year (2015) that Mother was a pretty stubborn and manipulating kid. She basically figured out what she wanted and made sure she could get it. She would get Margaret to buy her a candy bar with the offer to share it with Margaret. Margaret didn't know that it would really hurt Mother; she just knew Mother had money to buy it if she would do the purchasing. Then both girls got to eat it together.

  One story that denotes the effects of diabetes on my Mother was a Christmas that she was a sub in Tenaha schools. Mother had bought the sacks of nuts for Christmas morning and they were hidden on the top shelf in her closet. Joyce was snooping, found them, opened a sack and English walnuts spilled over the closet floor. She thought she got them all picked up. The next day at lunch, Mother felt something in her shoe, took it off, and found a walnut that she had worn all morning in her shoe. It had literally rubbed through the flesh down to the bone. That walnut cost Mother two weeks in the hospital with IV antibiotics, and surgery to remove one infected joint of her big toe. Of course, even there, you caught a glimpse of Mother...she made them re-write the permission paperwork before surgery that said the surgeon had permission to "remove any unnecessary body part" during surgery. She brought the surgeon into the room and explained that she, "was not born with any unnecessary parts, and if he needed to remove anything other than the one joint in the toe that was infected and would not heal, he would wake her up, they would discuss it, and then they would make that decision together!"

As Mother neared the end of her life, the diabetes really worked on her mind. It created a mean streak and altered her personality. There were days that no one in the family could do anything right. The blood sugar would be out of control, and she would say things that were a direct result of the disease itself. Looking back we could see it, but as a teenager in the house while it was going on, it was hard and we didn't always understand.

5. The Circle M

When I was two, Mother and Daddy bought 169 acres from Uncle Charles, one mile from Grandmother's house. They built a white frame, two-bedroom house that resembled Grandmother McDaniel's house in Tenaha. Here again, the memories flood my senses. Mother had a white kitchen with black ranch-style hinges on the cabinets. There was white tile with black fleck linoleum in the kitchen, and a tan fleck in the living room. The hallway and bedrooms had yellow pine plank floors. Two counter-top bars on either side separated the kitchen from the living room- now furnished with a tan western couch with embroidered split-rail fence topped with a western saddle on the back, a wagon wheel sided chair, and a wagon wheel coffee table. Even the curtains were covered with the pattern of bucking horses. Western was the theme. There was a short hallway leaving the living room with the most wonderful attic fan that made a repeating squeaky noise to sleep by, and my bedroom on the left and Mother and Daddy's bedroom on the right with the bathroom between the two. Our bathroom had no tub- just a shower, and when I smell Prell shampoo and Ivory soap it still takes me back. Outside was a single carport with an angled porch and utility/storage/work room. Always sitting on the end of the porch was a stack of wooden Coca-Cola cases because they always kept Cokes. This was not 5-6 cases; this was 12-15 cases per month. We drank enough Cokes that the Coca-Cola truck actually delivered to our house.

Just outside the backdoor was Cindy. We always had

a dog, and regardless of which dog it was, her name was always Cindy. They were always white and furry, and part Collie and Samoyed, until we moved to Center. Then we had one blonde dog...named Cindy, of course, that was Collie and mutt. We had a variety of cats from time to time- the orange striped and gray striped were always named Tiger, the black ones were either Cocoa or Midnight. We didn't name the rabbits because we had too many, and the horses were Flash and Barbara. Mother did name some of the cows- I remember Geneva had the longest tongue of any cow I'd ever seen, and she was one pest of a pet. She would have climbed up into the pick up if we had encouraged her at all.

Outside, we had a large rectangular yard. To the left of the driveway was a huge mulberry tree we climbed daily, and during the times they were getting ripe, we wore the purple juice stained fingers and lips that told what we had been eating. If Mother made us play outside until supper, the "free-will" tomato growing by the front water faucet or the mulberry was our salvation snacks until it was time to eat inside. To the left of that tree sat our swing set. The clothes line sat in the back left corner following the row of hedge along the fence. The rabbit hutch and the storage room filled the back left corner. There was a gate on the back fence, flanked on the right by a short row of narcissus that led outside into the pasture and the burn barrel. (Those narcissus came from Grandmother's, lived at the Circle M until I was twelve, Mother moved them to Center when we bought the house on Hwy 7, and eventually were moved to Harleton behind the den window when Mother and Daddy's place sold.) In the back right corner sat the well house and the gate that led into the garden on the right side. On the front right were the elevated gas barrels, and in the front yard was a silver leafed maple. At the end of the house was the TV antenna entwined with the most beautiful morning glories and below them were her violets and day lilies rounding the corner. Just past the corner of her bedroom, was the rose bed- and we actually dug up an arrowhead one spring when we were cleaning it out.

Mother and Daddy named their acreage the "Circle M" and had a large square metal, red and white sign designed and hung at the corner of our yard. They raised Hereford cattle, chickens, and Daddy bought a retired ranch horse named Flash that became my best friend in early childhood.

6. A Child's Christmas

The Christmas season began the first Sunday in December with our Christmas at Grandmother and Grandaddy Hancock's house. For years they had not put up a tree and it struck me as sad. When I was probably around eight years old, I discussed this with Mother and she said I could ask Grandmother and Grandaddy if we could put one up for them. They consented, and I felt better after that. The meal at Grandmother's was fabulous!! Everyone had their signature items to bring by the time I came along. Aunt Pauline would always bring a sliced ham, a relish tray with black olives, coconut pies, and rolls. Aunt Rosa Lee would always bring a chess pie and most of the time some deer sausage. Aunt June would bring a cherry nut cake, tuna salad sandwiches, and deviled eggs. Mother always made a fruit salad, and chocolate pies. Grandmother made chicken and dressing, fresh berry cranberry sauce, sweet potatoes, creamed potatoes, pecan pies, and the drinks. Everything we could think of was represented in this meal. All of the other items fluctuated from year to year- the vegetables, the other salads, and additional desserts. Those mentioned were just standard expectations and then all of the other items filled in. Everyone would arrive all during the morning, and the cousins would play in the yard and outbuildings all morning. We came in to inspect the progress in the kitchen and were outside again until the call to come eat. After lunch, Grandaddy gathered us all into the living room and Grandmother would read the list of grandchildren from her rocker as Grandaddy would pass out crisp $5.00 bills to each of the grandchildren. It was his big "todo" and he enjoyed every minute of it. Of course we knew it was a lot of money for a kid to get in that day, and next week we would answer to him as to what we did with it. The grand finale was always a statement from Grandaddy about how broke he was now that the grand kids got all his money! All in fun! It was that day that signaled the beginning of the Christmas season for me.

About two weeks before Christmas the decorations came out of the hall closet behind the hot water heater and those that could be put up early began to appear throughout the living room and kitchen. Daddy would go to the woods and cut pine limbs and attach on the eaves of the house and then staple the large outdoor lights on top. We could turn them on for only short periods of time because the limbs would dry out and the Christmas bulbs got hot, creating the possibility of a fire hazard. They were beautiful while they were turned on, and the smell of fresh pine was vivid on the front porch. As a child, I remember little things- like having a real Christmas tree that Mother and I would cut down each year. When Susan came along, she went too, as did John, and Joyce, and finally Alan. Mother loved Christmas. Daddy enjoyed watching it...but not participating in the majority of its activities. Whether it was raining (and I remember several Saturday's when it got time to go cut the tree that it was) or terribly cold, we anticipated the walk along the fence row or through the woods to the little pine or cedar that normally she had already spotted from a distance several weeks earlier. She always had more than one picked out, because upon close inspection, it may not be as shapely as it appeared from a distance, or a vine had covered the naked side. Of course, since it would sit in front of a picture window, it could have one bare side and it would still be fine. The ornaments were those of the 50's and 60's. Glass ornaments of mercury glass, large colored bulbs that did get hot and were a fire risk- thus the tree was only put up a week to 10 days before Christmas and the lights were only turned on at night for a couple of hours each night. We always had icicles that were put on one at a time to make the draped appearance- no throwing handfuls on at a time. We always thought it was gorgeous, no matter how straggly it really was. Several times I remember moving the coffee table under the window so we could use a smaller tree because we were living in such a small house.

We would always go to Tenaha and have Christmas Eve supper with Grandmother and Grandaddy McDaniel. Grandmother would make chicken and dressing and potatoes and she always had crème drops in the living room candy dish along with another dish of hard candy. I remember we had to wait for Grandaddy McDaniel to get off work from the truck stop across the road before we could eat supper and open gifts. We were all dancing at the road when he started crossing to come home! There was always a puzzle to work on in the dining room and after we ate, Michael would take all of the cousins outside and pop firecrackers. It was huge when we got old enough to pop them ourselves and not be strictly limited to the sparklers. Then we would come in and open presents. We would come home late after playing with Michael, Sharon and Linda Jo, and Gayla and Eddie, and so very tired which probably helped calm the excitement we had for the following morning.

Mother and Daddy always made sure Christmas was a big deal no matter how tight the money was that year. I don't know how they did it. I found out after I got grown that they barely made ends meet- and that was with a garden, farm beef, and an occasional pig. I thought that was the way we were supposed to be in the country and the best meals to this day are the simple country eating I grew up on. I never realized that we were poor. Mother always made cookies at Christmas- not chocolate chip, but molasses and fruitcake cookies. We put up a gumdrop tree and Susan and I would get to put the gumdrops on for it to sit on the kitchen bar. The big tree always had candy canes incorporated with the ornaments, but Daddy was the only one that could eat one before Christmas morning.

I do remember a few of the gifts from Christmas. One year we got the first dog, Cindy. One year Susan and I both got new dolls and pink wooden homemade doll beds. A couple of years we got doll buggies and I remember a pink, wooden doll high chair. Then one year after we moved to Center Santa brought me a money tree. Christmas was always celebrated on Christmas morning- Santa and presents.

We were always up early and searching for a pile of unwrapped gifts from Santa for each of us kids, and a row of rolled down large paper grocery sacks with bags of candy or nuts stuffed in them all that lined one wall. There was always a package of Malted Milk Balls, Milky Ways, Baby Ruth bars, candy Orange Slices, a package of Ribbon candy (I think it was for Daddy because we honestly didn't like it), Crème Drops, M &M's, sometimes Hershey bars, and whatever else was available at the time. There was always one sack that had nothing but the large bags of nuts in it- English walnuts, mixed nuts, almonds, Brazil nuts, etc. Some years as we would crack the English walnuts, there would be quarters inside instead of the nuts. That was such an extra treat! Santa always included a sack of oranges and grapefruit, as well as a fresh coconut that we poked holes in to pour out the coconut milk. Then we took a hammer and broke it in order to eat the meat. We never did have stockings as we grew up. Santa just brought us that stuff in bulk!!! Then we opened the often cheap little gifts we had purchased at the Carthage Five and Dime (Ben Franklin's) as a final mix of pride and excitement in being able to pick out and pay for the gifts we gave by ourselves.

One year I was beginning to doubt whether Santa was real or not, and Mother and Daddy got someone to play the part, come early before we went to bed on Christmas Eve, and deliver all our gifts while we were watching. Of course we questioned the reason for the truck and why the sleigh and reindeer were not there. The answer was simple... can't have a sleigh without snow- which we never had at Christmas. So he got a pickup when he got far enough south that the snow played out. After he delivered all the gifts, we were made to sit in his lap and tell him thank you and give him a thank you kiss. I had never kissed anyone with facial hair before, and thought that was majorly gross. I still do not like it to this day. However, I did go back to school with the affirmation that he was real, and I think that even my teacher was amazed at what had transpired that year at our house! I think that regardless how difficult the year had been, Mother and Daddy always wanted our Christmas to be magical. And it was! To this day I still want it to be magical for my kids and grand kids...and will go to extremes to create some surprise or out of the ordinary event to help it be so. Like Mother, I want it to be a special memory that doesn't get pushed aside but is revered as a very happy family time together.

7. Other Holidays

Valentine's Day was Daddy's special day to bring us a box of candy while we were little. As we got older, he gave up that tradition, and I don't know why. It could have been that there were too many of us and money was tight, he didn't know what to get John, Mother didn't need the temptation of any more candy in the house, or because Mother told him it was unnecessary. Whatever the reason, we enjoyed the treat while it lasted.

Easter was a very special holiday when we were little. It took Mother and Grandmother sometimes together to get us dolled up for Sunday morning on Easter. We always had the little stiff ruffled petticoats of the early 60's. We wore little white gloves, had new white patent leather shoes, ruffled socks, little hats, and a new white purse. All of this accessorized the new dresses that Mother and Grandmother had made us. One year Mother stayed up all night before Easter completing the cross-stitch embroidery on our purple and white gingham dresses. She had rows of triangles of embroidery around the hemline and across the bodice of our dresses, matching the size of the triangles so they came out exact at the hemline of a gathered skirt!

We had three egg hunts each year- the big one at Woods church the Saturday preceding Easter. All of the kids in both communities of Woods and Old Center came and we were divided into age groups to help make it fair. The actual day of Easter, we would have one at our house for Susan and me, and then we would go to Grandmother McDaniel's for the last one. Most of the time, Michael, Sharon, and Linda Jo would also hunt at that one.

8. Sharing a Bedroom

Susan and I shared the bedroom initially. We had a double bed, and we always rolled a blanket to split the middle. I didn't want her on my side, and she didn't want me on hers. On a trip to Austin for a Highway Department meeting one summer, Daddy brought us back little gray schnauzer stuffed dogs that we sat on the head of the bookcase headboard on either side. Since both of us had our own closets, I really don't remember us fighting over things. We both had our own interests. I collected rocks and moss, coins, and an occasional doll. We played pretty well together. I had to remember to never leave my dolls out because if there was a pair of scissors within 100 feet, any doll got a haircut from Susan.

When I was 7 and Susan was 4, Daddy's brother Michael moved in for a year. Grandaddy McDaniel was diagnosed with TB and was in the Tyler TB hospital during that time. Grandmother McDaniel was trying to run the Shamrock Cafe by herself and was hitting the bottle again during that time, so Michael came to stay with us. We sat up a roll-a-way bed in the corner of our bedroom for him. I remember he had a collection of little metal airplanes that were off limits for Susan and me.

Mother did let me decide on the color of the walls and curtains in our room- bright red walls, and sheer white overlapping curtains. We also had a white chenille bedspread. Imagine that with two little country girls! White!?! There were several times when the sun was coming in through the windows just right that the reflection from the red walls made anyone in the living room come look. It looked like our room was on fire. When we moved to the rent house in Center, Susan and I had twin beds in the middle bedroom, and John had the full size bed in the back bedroom. Then when we moved to the house on Hwy. 7, I got to move into my own room.

9. Raising Chickens in Texas

Grandmother was a wise woman. She was responsible for the chicken industry being in Texas. She had read about chickens being raised for commercial use in Arkansas and convinced Grandaddy to build her several houses with yards that would hold 600 chickens each. That would be part of her income. They began to raise chickens which took 15-18 weeks to reach maturity. Mother helped with this adventure and would go to Tenaha, take the flatbed truck, unload a boxcar of chicken feed in 50 pound sacks, bring it home and unload it. One time Grandaddy fussed about Mother wearing blue jeans to complete this feat. Mother's reply came after she had to change a flat on the road between Tenaha and the house. She confronted Grandaddy with, "Well I guess I would have looked real cute trying to change a flat on the highway in a dress." Grandaddy never fussed about Mother wearing jeans again.

When it was time to feed each day, they would go to the feed room, move the sacks that needed to be used, and then carry them to the feeders. She was feeding chickens, moving those sacks the day she kicked into labor with me. Later Grandmother and Grandaddy built chicken houses that would house 1500-3000 and didn't have yards. When Mother and Daddy built theirs, they built the largest in Shelby County at the time. It housed 13,000 chickens, and by then they were maturing at 9 weeks. Of course, now, no one will build anything less than 100,000 capacity and they now sell at 6 weeks. The year that Grandaddy died, he was presented with a certificate acknowledging him as the first commercial chicken grower in Texas.

While we lived on the Circle M, I remember getting up early and going with Mother to the chicken house. In the winter Susan and I had blue jeans lined with red plaid flannel. When we got to the chicken house, Mother would raise a brooder about halfway up and we would sit under it to keep warm. She would go about the necessary work to be done- washing the water troughs with a rag pushed by a stick to make sure the shavings were not going to clog it and make the water run over and then make "cake" which would stink to the high heavens. She would walk through the house and pick up the dead chickens (they have a tendency to sit down and smother each other by sitting too close to each other at night, or if there is a thunder shower- even if they have the lights left on.) She would walk the feed troughs and make sure the feed hopper let the feed down- sometimes it would clog in the outside hopper and wouldn't feed into the automatic feeder that went around the house. Sometimes it would be a rat that had gotten in and got caught when it turned a corner and clogged it up. Occasionally there would be a snake to kill, or wolves to shoot outside that had come up too close. The stench that is associated with chicken litter is something that you do become accustomed to if you live close by, but even to this day when I drive through an area that raises chickens, it still is stout on the nose. We have walked many miles raising flaps, lowering flaps, calming chickens during a storm, checking on waterers and feed troughs, and picking up dead chickens.

Raising chickens wasn't all bad, though. It really did have exciting moments. Getting ready for baby chicks was always fun to kids. Dump truck loads of fresh shavings were brought in the chicken house and it smelled absolutely wonderful!!! Mother always hired one or two of the neighbors to come help spread them with a rake and that was an all day job! Then the babies would arrive on the baby chicken truck. They would unload pasteboard petitioned boxes with yellow fuzzy chicks that transitioned a quiet chicken house into a cheeping nursery that only hushed during sudden moments of unexpected loud interrupting noise. Then we got excited by the occasional chicken snake, discovery of a nest of rats, or washing of the water jars when the chicks got big enough to reach the waterers. There were the sudden thunderstorms and a mad dash to lower the outside flaps to keep the rain from blowing in, and the trips to walk the chickens if the electricity went out at night because the chickens would sit...and then smother each other as they would congregate in groups. We kids really anticipated the delivery of the propane for the tank out front of the chicken house. I don't know if we were so poor that the driver felt sorry for Susan and me, or if he just had a big heart. Either way, he always brought us a complete box of the large (only size there was back then) Baby Ruth bars!! For two little country girls that didn't go to the store every day, it was almost Christmas when he arrived. He would always pick on us, tease us a little, but it was all in fun. Then of course the biggest day when you raise chickens is when you load them to go to the processing plant. We called it "chicken catching night." It was a rough type of person that would work all night catching and loading chickens. It was not a high paying job- probably on the very bottom of the pay scale. It was known that several, if not all of the catchers would come half drunk, and would cuss a blue streak all night. It definitely was not a place for two little blonde-headed girls to spend the night. Mother didn't have babysitters...and I don't remember Grandmother coming over to help out during those times, I guess because she had her own chickens to worry about. We went to the chicken house with Mother and sometimes Daddy. Since Daddy worked in Center the next day and had the drive, and because the chickens were Mother's job, she was the one that went...and we went with her. To make sure everything stayed under control, Mother strapped on her loaded pistol and away we would go. She was known in all the circles of the chicken business as the "lady with the gun." She only had to speak once, and what she said- went. She could eliminate the cussing and could send any drunk on his way. We grew up thinking that was completely normal. No one messed with my mother or daddy. Mother had the gun, and Daddy had been a wrestler and was strong as an ox and still looked the part. Either way, we were two protected little girls in a setting that was probably less than safe, but was insured to be safe, simply because it would be no other way with them there.

10. Life on the Circle M

Mother and Daddy were really a team in their endeavors. Daddy would crank up the Ford tractor and plow up the place for the garden, and all of us would fertilize, and plant. We would pull weeds and get ant bit (before the dreaded fire ant though), but we also knew at an early age the sound of the bobwhite that always nested under the end peach tree, and that the fresh English peas were really tasty eaten fresh-picked and raw right there in the garden. We walked to the blackberry bushes on the left end of the garden waiting impatiently until the tame berries were ripe for the picking, and we loved the feel of the fresh dirt mixed with just dug new potatoes. Mother and Daddy had several pecan trees with plank fences built around them to keep the horse and cows from eating the leaves. These adorned the outside of the yard fence. Mother liked the farm and ranching. Daddy liked the cowboy idea that easily could get associated with the ranching end. He bought a retired ranch horse- a brown and white paint that he called Flash. By the time I could sit on Flash, his "flash" was just about gone! I do remember Daddy riding him to round up the cows, him positioning me in the middle of the road to help turn the cows into the new pasture as he was moving them from one to the next. It never occurred to me that one could actually hurt me. I moved my arms up and down and made the noises I had seen and heard the adults make, and the cows always turned, and Daddy rode up in the rear. I loved Flash, though. I could catch him anywhere, lead him to any fence, and then climb on. I would ride him bareback with no lead rope or bridle and when I got through riding, I would slip off and let him go. If I was barefoot- which was most of the summer, I knew where the grass burrs, thistles, and bull nettles were, and I better be prepared to walk gingerly, or tough it out to get back to the house. Flash taught me a lot about horses. The smell of a horse and the nuzzle of a horse hunting a snack are still some of my favorite comforts even now. There is something totally relaxing about sitting on a horse and meandering through a pasture. Flash also taught me that a trained horse is something of great value. It was a good thing that as a youngster Flash was old and getting more arthritic because I would have gotten hurt if he would have gone as fast as I wanted him to. As a child, I asked for and was given a Shetland pony for my birthday one year. Barbara was as stubborn as any horse could be. She was hard to catch, and harder to ride. When we would ride to Grandmother and Granddaddy's house, we had to cross a creek. At that time it had a wooden bridge and there was no way I could get Barbara on that bridge to cross. When she began to smell water she started trying to bolt and turn around and run back to the house. She gave me my one crying spell on a horse when she bolted with me and ran back into a barbwire fence before she stopped. I was so mad I could have popped. I would rather ride Flash any day. In fact, after that event, Daddy would stop and swap horses with me until we got over the bridge and then he would swap back. Of course, coming home she didn't bother stopping at the bridge. She would cross it and then try running the other ½ mile home. She had several colts- and I got to sell them, or give one or two to Susan, but I never really bonded with her like I did Flash.

    The Circle M had so many wonderful memories. I

remember when we dug the big pond. That was such a huge event for any kid. I remember the bulldozers working in the hot summer and when they killed their motor for the day, Daddy would turn us loose. Barefoot in fresh dug dirt that sloped downward, we could run forever before we began to run uphill on the other side. Oh, and it smelled incredibly fresh! Every day we were there when the work day was over and we played until dark. We saw the spillway pipe and the dam being built, we knew that the property line was in line with the pipe. Mother and Daddy taught us those things even when we were very young. The creek was the line once you walked straight back from the pond dam. I was between 4-6 when that was built, and we had such great memories at that pond. When I was in elementary, Daddy built a picnic table on our side of the pond out of huge round posts and old highway wooden signs. It would seat 12-15 people. We had a fire pit dug-in the very location it sits today, and Mother set out wisteria and yellow jasmine vine. Daddy found a wild huckleberry bush and we would pick it every year until it died after I got grown. We swam in the pond- as kids we had the little bubble romper swim suits and Daddy would tie a rope around our belly and then to the boat tied to a tree there. We couldn't wander off, and we couldn't wade out too deep, and he knew where we were at all times. We loved it. We fished, skipped rocks, had camp outs, wiener roasts, and numerous picnics there. We picked dewberries in the edges of the meadows coming to the pond, and my 5th grade sleepover birthday party ended with a breakfast cookout at the pond with every girl in my class there. Daddy planted crimson clover and purple vetch in the front meadow coming into the pond several springs and the cows simply loved it. It truly was a happy place for a child to grow up.

As a younger child, I could roam to the little pond immediately behind our house. Mother and Daddy had a little wooden duck house back there and we had tame ducks from time to time. I remember the snakes in the little pond. In fact, one spring, Flash was at the yard fence, I was barefoot, and I led him over to the barbwire yard fence, and climbed on for a morning ride. It was nice weather, so I rode him down behind the little pond dam. There were always wild violets in the spring back there and the most beautiful ferns anyone could imagine. Sure enough, the violets were in bloom, and I slid off Flash. He meandered off, and I picked violets, and started around the corner where the pond overflowed at the spillway. I had made the turn and about 20 feet on the front side of the pond, I felt something really cold, and it was moving under my foot. I looked down to discover I had just stepped barefoot, right behind the head, of a water moccasin. He was glaring at me and I knew when I moved that foot he would waste no time in striking. I took a breath and ran! I know that there were a ton of stickers between me and the house, but I didn't feel a one! I was one scared little girl!

From time to time, Grandmother McDaniel would come fish both ponds. She loved to pole fish. Sometimes she would bring one of her sisters with her; sometimes she would come alone. She always seemed to enjoy a stringer or bucket full of perch to take back home. Occasionally she would catch a bass or catfish, but most of the time is was white perch. I never really got into the fishing. There was always something else that caught my eye, something to explore, or something else to do. I don't hate it, I just like other things more, I guess.

Daddy had the idea one year that we should raise

rabbits for another meat source. He built a four pen rabbit hutch. It was so sturdy, it was used then, later when we moved to Center, and then I moved it to Harleton when we built on Hardyhill. He got several does and a couple of bucks, and we were in business. He put a couple of small nail kegs in with the does, and when they began to pull the front tufts of hair, we knew there would be babies before long. Some of the does were more protective or sensitive than others, so we knew to leave them alone until the babies began to explore outside of their nest. Others were more tolerant, and we always had to sneak a peak of the newborns when we could. They multiplied quite well, and quite often we would take the "fryers" out and have a rabbit "dressing." I learned early how to hold them while Daddy ringed all four feet, cut along the center front line, and pulled the fur off in one piece. Mother would wash them and package for the freezer, and we would have two or three fried for supper that night. They tasted like white meat from chicken, and it really was good! (Dustin didn't understand after his first squirrel hunt years later how I knew how to dress the squirrel while Richard was tied up painting the school field house. Oh Dustin, there were lots of things you may not have known about your mother!)

  Uncle Charles and Aunt June lived across a pasture in front of our house. Their garden and the blacktop road were between our house and theirs. They had a huge white frame house that was up on probably four foot pillars. They had a washroom built around the well out back, but my favorite envy was their bathtub. It was a huge claw-footed tub. We had a shower- no tub- so a tub bath was a really big treat. I knew that right after supper each night, Aunt June would run their kids through the tub and if I was there, well...I could persuade Aunt June to let me take a bath with Nettie Mae, too. Hence, the reason that I ran away several late afternoons and Mother would have to call Aunt June to see if I had made it to their bathtub. I really did get into a lot of trouble for leaving without telling Mother where I was going...even though she knew exactly where I was going to be. I finally told Uncle Charles that if they ever remodeled the bathroom, I wanted the tub. Sure enough, after I married and we moved to Harleton, he gave me the tub and we turned it into a reading loveseat for our kids when they were little.

Lots of things change quickly with time. Others take a little more time to evolve. The utilities then were very similar to those today in rural East Texas. When we lived on the Circle M, we had a well. The little white well house sat in the back corner of the yard and occasionally Daddy would have to wrap the pump so it wouldn't freeze in the winter, or work on the pump if it started pulling in sand. At one point, he decided to plant a little flower garden beside the well house. We planted blue and pink bachelor buttons, wisteria in the sweet gum tree, roses, and bluebonnets. We spent quite a bit of time putting down brick as the outlines for the pathways and filling the pathways with gravel. He even set up a little fountain using a Texas cutout of granite he had cut when they designed the sign for the Highway Department in Center where he was now working. When we cleaned out the storage room in order to sell Mother and Daddy's place in Center, I found one of those cutouts and brought it to the house.

We also had a black rotary phone on a party line that sat on the bar. If you picked up the phone and anyone was using it, you could sit and listen to their conversations. Most of the time you could hear when they picked up or put it down, so you knew to be careful when talking about anyone on the phone. Our phones only had to dial the one prefix number and the last four digits so our number was Cherry 8-3456. Everyone that was on a particular party line had their distinct ring as well. Two short rings, a long and short ring, etc. were for different folks. We learned which one was ours and who was on the line getting a call as well.

    Electricity was as dependable in my childhood as it is now. In the winter, there would always be a time during ice storms that we would be without. Fortunately, we had butane heaters and stove, so we never were without warmth or the means to cook. We kept oil lamps for light, and managed just like we would today.

11. Grandaddy's Beans

We followed Grandmother and Grandaddy many miles across their place during my childhood. There were so many lessons they taught me without ever saying a word. One in particular had to do with the seasons of life. Grandaddy had no clue at the time, but this lesson about his beans impacted me like few others.

Grandaddy would start plowing the sandy soil in several large fields getting ready to plant in early spring. I vaguely remember a mule in my youngest years, but shortly thereafter he worked his fields with a tractor. He would disappear from the house and come back hot and sweaty after plowing for hours. Then he would make the rows, open them, fertilize, and the close the rows and wait the remainder short time until it was time to plant. Then we would all be allowed to follow him and walk the rows (between them only- and if you stepped over, you better step waaay over), and count and drop the seeds in the holes that Grandmother or Grandaddy were digging immediately in front of us. We knew that for peas/beans, we were to drop four seed. Then someone would come right behind us, and cover the seed, and lightly tamp the hole with three hoe taps. We would hope for rain, and shortly after wards Grandaddy would be back in the fields with a hoe, the remaining seed to fill in where a hill didn't sprout.

Many more trips to the field followed. Grandaddy would come in at lunch hot and sweaty with his bandana wiping his forehead, overalls wet with sweat. He had weeded all morning with the hoe, walking and working row after row. After eating lunch, and lying down in the hall for about an hour under the attic fan, he would disappear again to the field. These were trips we didn't make. I think partially because we might be more destructive to the rows than helpful, and partially because this was Grandaddy's pride and joy.

When the peas or beans began to bloom, we would get the report that it looked like we might get a decent crop this year. Then a little later, he would appear with a couple of small pods, and we all knew the harvest was fast approaching. As they filled out, he would come in with a handful, and then the first bucket-full. Within a week or so, it was bushel baskets. Then we spent hours under the China berry tree shelling peas or beans, followed by Grandmother spending hours washing, blanching, and freezing or canning in order to save for the winter.

Here is where the novelty began for me. While we were shelling, Grandaddy would carefully remove some of the bigger, more filled out pods of peas and set them down beside his red metal lawn chair. These selected beans/peas would make their way onto the back porch and were spread on newspapers there to dry. Every time we would shell beans, a few more were added to the pile on the back porch. By the end of the summer Grandaddy had a fairly good pile of the best of the crop, dried, and waiting to be shelled.

I knew that before long we would be given the job to get the window sticks (sticks that held the bedroom windows open so they wouldn't fall since there was no air conditioning), one of Grandmother's white sheets, and come to the yard beside the cellar. The house made an "L" by the cellar as the carport jutted out in front of their bedroom window. There would be no cross breeze, so the beans/peas would be protected. Grandaddy would then position whichever grand kids were there around the edges of Grandmother's white sheet that he had carefully spread on the ground. He poured the dried beans/peas in the center of the sheet, then we were all handed a window stick, and we threshed. We beat the dried shells with our window sticks, which broke open, and the seeds were caught by the sheet underneath. When Grandaddy was sure we had gotten most of the seeds out, he would gather the hulls, and throw over the fence under the oak that stood there. He would get quart jars, gather up his seed, and fill his jars with the best seed for next year's crop. He then would take them to the back porch and put them in the large freezer to keep until the following spring. Every year I remember him repeating this procedure.

    Grandaddy knew the seasons, what must be done to prepare for each, and the work that went with each season he genuinely embraced. He knew to pace himself in order to accomplish the task that to me seemed more than overwhelming- in size and work, but he never slacked at any phase of the cycle. That was why we always had peas/beans to eat. He was never wasteful and he protected what he had, but he then gave generously from his hard work. Oh, the life lessons from Grandaddy's beans!

12. Mother and Daddy's Hobbies

Sunday afternoons were special as a youngster growing up. Mother and Daddy had several paint by number kits that they took out and worked on occasionally. They were the hard ones that they would work on for months before they were finished and eventually some of these completed paintings made their way to the walls of our house. Sometimes they would buy the easy ones for me to paint along with them, and I loved it. About once a month, Sunday would mean that we would load up and take a drive. Nowhere in particular, but we would discuss the hay crop, the new paint job on someone's house, the magnolia tree blooms, or the need for rain. We always enjoyed the ride. Daddy and Mother would play forty-two with Aunt June and Uncle Charles or the neighbors up the road on a Saturday night from time to time. Mother spent some of her spare time sewing- but I know it was from necessity and not so much from enjoyment. We did have some cute "look alike" dresses, though, and some she embroidered for the finishing touches. They did collect coins when I was a kid. We have several blue coin books and we would spend a Sunday afternoon looking for pennies, nickels, or quarters to fill those books. At that particular time, we would take in a bucket of coins to the bank and they would exchange it for a different bucket. Collecting coins wasn't that popular, so the banks didn't go through them first to weed out the good ones.

13. We Were Poor

The novelty about growing up poor is that we didn't know it. Food was never a problem while we were growing up. Garden vegetables were abundant; there was always a beef in the freezer, sometimes a pig, and always several chickens. So when Mother told me as a teen about a year that they were too poor to visit the grocery store for anything other than bare basics, I was shocked. She reminded me of a year when we ate biscuits and sausage, with ribbon cane syrup for supper most nights. It is one of my favorite meals...and I still think it reminds me of a wonderful childhood. Mother and Daddy never dwelt on the things that we didn't have, they focused on what blessings we had. I think because they worked non-stop to provide for us and did not depend on any hand-out, it biased my thinking in that area. Most of us can do far more than we do. From my observation, government assistance is much abused and encouraged in this country, and because of that very thing, we have lost the pride, creativity, and satisfaction in providing for family through hard work. It does not take a world of "things" to make a family happy.

14. Working Alongside

When we outgrew our clothes, Mother would fold them up in large, brown grocery bags and deliver them to Talmidge and their family that lived on a small place that shared our back boundary. They had a bunch of kids, and lived in a small square two bedroom house. I don't know at what point they got running water, but I saw her drawing water from the well several times while passing. From time to time, Talmidge would hire out to iron clothes or clean house with Mother, and sometimes her oldest boys would help us clean chicken houses and spread shavings. They were a hard-working family and didn't mind working alongside others that were working hard as well.

Lola Bea was another black lady that lived on Grandaddy's place. She would come over from time to time and hire out to do ironing, too. Her husband, Ernest, helped Grandaddy with jobs on his place- building fence, working in the barn, etc. in exchange for living in the little house on the place. They occupied the unpainted house at the end of the cedar flanked lane across from the church. They also had a house full of kids, but Grandmother and Grandaddy never seemed to see skin color, so we were never brought up to be prejudiced like I have seen some, especially in East Texas. Every time I saw Lola Bea, we shared hugs, and we thought it was just as special for her to be at our house as it was any white neighbor that came. She was always appreciative for the opportunity to earn wages, and Mother was always appreciative for someone to help her.

There was a mutual respect between families and a sense of community- regardless of race. That is not true in most East Texas areas...and probably was not even throughout our community, but we were raised to get along and respect all people and skin color was never an issue. I remember stories of one winter when some of Lola Bea's family was ill, and Grandmother cooked for them, bought and delivered medicine, and nursed them back to health. I also remember a story where one of the black ladies served as a wet nurse to a white family when the new mother didn't produce milk and the baby would have died without help.

I do know that there is a fine line between respect, culture, and prejudice. A lot of that understanding has to do with a person's interpretation, the time frame in history, and the tone of the situation. When Grandaddy had people working for him, his hired hands always ate on the back porch. The kids ran back and forth from back porch to kitchen where Grandaddy and Grandmother ate trying to hear both sets of conversation during the meal. We thought it a privilege when Grandmother asked us to take out the tea for refills or take dessert out to the folks on the porch. We didn't look at that as prejudice. On ranches with all white hired hands, the same concept was in place. That was respect for the owner's home. Everyone was grateful to Grandmother for the meal- black or white, and the tone of the situation was always relaxed, cordial, and gracious.

Voluntary integration began the year I was in first grade in Carthage. The black school between Tenaha and Carthage eventually was shut down and those children began attending Carthage schools. I really didn't realize what emotions that point had for some until we moved to Center and I got older. Even then, the most hurtful things said, for both sides, came from adults, not the kids.

When we moved to Center, Mother took some classes from SFA one summer, and we were introduced to Miss Ida. She was the black lady that would babysit us while Mother was gone to class. That was two days a week, and Miss Ida would always cook us cornbread and dirty rice. Once she had cooked it for us the first time, it was a request every week. Susan and I both learned that recipe from her and still use it today.

I think there were several reasons that prejudice was never an issue. Respect, honesty, equality, and work ethic all were key in not letting prejudice have a foothold. Grandmother always had a work ethic no one could argue with. She never asked someone to do something that she was not doing herself. Mother grew up with that work ethic as well. I have tried to do that in my family.

15. Company

We loved having friends and family come to visit from time to time. "Little Mary," one of Grandaddy Hancock's cousins came to stay with us a week a couple of times every year. Mother explained that she truly had so much less than we did, and Mary considered it a treat to come for that week. I remember that she always brought Mother a little gift as a thank you for the visit. One time she brought a dozen dime store washcloths. She was so proud of that gift. I can only imagine that she skimped and saved in order to buy that for us. Even as a kid it made such a strong impression. Mary always talked way too loud and too much, and everyone was tired when she went back home. She had never learned to drive, and had never owned a car. She loved to go...anywhere. She always wanted one of us kids to scratch her back- odd request, but one of us always obliged.

Norma and her two girls, Donna Kay and Pam, would always come through during the summer, and we loved playing with cousins we were not around all the time. They lived in Belle Chase, Louisiana, and got to attend parties where they actually bought party dresses. When they came, they always brought boxes of outgrown clothes, and we dug around in those boxes hoping we would come across a "party dress" that Mother would let us have for dress-up. Susan and I played "princess" for months after we would discover such treasures!

Lots of times, family would come to Grandmother and Grandaddy's house and we would all gather there for the visits. I remember Aunt Grace's laughter, Uncle

Carroll's teasing, Aunt Clara Bunyard's icebox coconut cake, Aunt Lucy's generous hugs, as well as Aunt Clara Hancock's short and stern stature. When family came for visits, it was simply a phone call away from us joining the fun.

Occasionally we would gather elsewhere. I remember all of the cousins gathering at Aunt Rosa Lee's house once. I was probably the youngest there. Rodney, Ralph, Gary Don, Gloria, Shirley, Alice, Jr., and Nettie Mae were all there, and we got to go to the A&W for lunch and order hamburgers and root beer floats. That was such a huge treat, the memory just stuck!

Oh, and my favorite Uncle Emory and Aunt Martha memory was one summer night when it was just Susan and me as kids. Uncle Charles and his bunch, Linda Sue, Rose Anne, Aunt Pauline, Uncle Jens, and Kay, and our bunch, were at Uncle Emory's for a swim party and he grilled hamburgers. I had never gotten to swim in a pool at night, and the smell of the hamburgers grilling was wonderful! He had a bicycle built for two, and Mother and Daddy went on a night-time ride and on their way back, we saw them, and got to ride as well. It was a splendid night!

Throughout the year we looked forward to the times the neighbor kids would come over, too. Tim Harrigan would come and we played outside a lot. He was rough and tough, and we got along well. He rode his bike over when he got old enough, and we would ride bikes up and down the black top road for hours. Pam Edge would come from time to time and play with Susan and me. Her Mom would take us to Carthage to the movies occasionally, and on one of the trips home from the show, she treated us to our very first chocolate dipped ice cream cone. By the time I was in the 5th grade, Debbie Edge from Old Center would ride her bike over and we would play until late. Then she would get on her bike and ride the 3+ miles home. She also sat on the bus with me coming home from school and introduced me to a couple of different snacks- powdered Tang by the spoonfuls, and chinquapins that she had gathered from the Sabine River bottom.

    We were never bored. We always found things or folks to entertain us. We took advantage of every situation. Uncle Charles worked on and drove a maintainer for the county. He always parked it in front of his house across the road. We tried almost daily to catch him before he got to the house, and ride the last 200 yards with him home on that thing. Simple things were our treasures.

16. Birthdays

Birthdays were special at our house growing up. We didn't have parties every year, but Mother made a point of making sure we had 2-3 presents and she always cooked our favorite meal. My all-time favorite as a child was fried chicken or chicken fried steak, creamed potatoes with gravy, peas, carrot and pineapple salad, and a chocolate cake with chocolate frosting. Nettie, Alice, Shirley, and sometimes Gloria would come over for some special birthday gathering. I do remember Mother buying plastic swans that were candy holders as favors one year for my birthday. The only gift I can remember in particular was the year that Mother and Daddy allowed me to get a Shetland pony. Mr. Robertson from Center brought out a load of ponies and set up temporary panels at the corner of the pasture. As they circled within the pen, I got to sit on the fence and choose the one I wanted, thus Barbara came to live at the Circle M.

When I was in the 5th grade, Mother and Daddy gave permission for me to invite all the girls in my entire 5th grade class to my house for a sleepover. They came, and we had kids sleeping under the table, on the couch, in the closets, on both mattresses (we took my bed apart), and anywhere else they could literally find room to stretch out. We played all over the place, riding the one axle trailer as a seesaw, riding Flash, exploring the barn and chicken house, playing board games, and finally the next morning, walking over to the pond for Daddy to cook breakfast outdoors on the fire pit. Since we moved to Center after the 5th grade, I didn't see some of these kids again until we met again at Panola, seven-eight years later. I remember Debbie Joines telling me then that the sleepover in the 5th grade was her favorite memory of elementary school!! Nothing like taking some city kids and initiating them to the country!!

After we moved to Center, on my 16th birthday, my best friends, Jan Mahan, Terri Russell, and Naomi Green threw me a surprise swim birthday party. They decorated the picnic table in the swim area with streamers, bought a huge sheet cake, and probably 20-25 of my friends came to have burgers, cake, and swim. That was special.

17. Toys

When we were young, Susan and I got red and white trikes one year for Christmas, and one year we each got a pedal car. Mine was blue and white. We had a little red wagon. After a rain that filled it one summer afternoon, I climbed in, took off all my clothes, and took a bath in the nude out in the yard. Mother never said that was cute...but she did get it on silent movies.

One year as I got older, I wanted a Barbie and Mother thought they were ugly, so she let me have a Tammy doll instead. When I was 10 or 11, I got a portable hair dryer and thought I had entered the world of teenagers. One year after we got old enough to ride, we got bikes. Mine was blue and white. I had watched enough circuses on TV that I thought it important to learn to balance standing up on the seat without holding the handlebars. It can be done...I think 15 seconds was my record, and on a blacktop road with potholes as well!! And no, we didn't use helmets. It is a wonder any of us got grown without getting killed.

My first water gun was a royal blue water rifle, which I got on vacation when I was six on the way to Yellowstone. When I was 4-5, at one of the Highway Department meetings, I was chosen to draw for the door prize that night. The gift for doing that was a play Doctor's kit. I was elated because I wanted to become a doctor, even at that age. They apologized to me numerous times because it should have been a nurse's kit for a little girl. Girls became nurses, boys became doctors. Little did they realize it was the perfect gift for me.

One Christmas I got a pogo stick and jumped on that thing all the way to the mailbox and back several times. Sometimes we would pick out little toys at the Perry Bro. Five and Dime in Center. The toys were always on the far right aisle in Center and on the far left aisle at the Ben Franklin's in Carthage, all the way to the back of the store. Little tea sets always caught my eye, as well as little sets of dishes. One time, Kay brought her old toys to Grandmother's for the cousins to play with. She brought a toy stove and refrigerator. We didn't know such things even existed. Susan and I played with those for hours at a time.

Toys were always associated with special events or holidays. Rarely did we get a toy just because we were shopping but we would pick them out and wish while we were at the grocery or the dime store. Most of the time we learned to use what we had around us for our toys. We picked weeds that grew in our yard, tore them up, and played like it was turnip greens in old pans that Mother no longer used. We climbed the rabbit hutch after Daddy moved it out of the yard and into the pasture underneath a huge field pine. Then we climbed on up into the field pine and shimmied down the limbs and rode them like spring horses. We rode the butane tank like a horse as well. We made roads out of the embankments by the road in the red clay for a bike trail, made a ton of mud pies and dried them on an old board or on the end of the slide or swing seats, chased rabbits without success- but Shirley and Alice could catch them so we kept on trying, and played dress up with hand-me-down party dresses sent in care packages from Norma's girls, Donna Kay and Pam. We made play bows and arrows and one summer Daddy helped us sew burlap feed sacks together and we built a teepee taller than the house, that would seat 15-20 kids. Shirley, Alice, and Nettie helped with that project. We tried to make our dog perform as a circus dog with no luck, and we played hospital-writing play prescriptions just like we would see the doctor do when we visited him for checkups. Daddy hung the horse saddles from rope off the rafters in the tractor shed, so it was an automatic rope swing if we were exploring at the barn. We did all the little things, too, like blow dandelions or run our finger down the leaves of the little plant that made the rose colored balls. The leaves would automatically curl up and was always a distraction to whatever we were doing at the time.

18. Signs of the Times

Things have changed quite a bit during my lifetime. TV, radio, shopping, and the value of money have all taken various paths, for sure. As a young child, TV was in black and white. We had a square TV that sat on a roller stand with a cloth front. It sat in the corner of the living room. We anticipated watching the Lone Ranger, and Roy Rogers as our favorite shows with horses. Dr. Ben Casey, and Dr. Kildare were our favorite doctor shows, and Saturday morning was full of cartoons such as Mickey Mouse, Donald Duck, Foghorn Leghorn, Yogi Bear, and Bugs Bunny. All of that began with a non-cartoon, Tarzan, at 6:30AM. There was no way we could sleep late on Saturdays. It was our favorite time of the week and the only time as youngsters that we could eat in front of the TV. We also loved shows like I love Lucy, and Andy Griffith. The Real McCoys was another favorite. I wished I could have seen the Munsters, but that came on Wednesday night and we always were at church. I hated The Twilight Zone, and even though we were sent to bed when it came on, the music made it super hard to go to sleep while it played throughout the show. The shows were strictly for entertainment then, and even Hollywood had a little moral standard- a far cry from the programs that are shown today.

As a teenager, Saturday night always kicked off with HeeHaw. We watched Hawaii 5-O, and the detective shows such as Matlock took over TV. Happy Days and Laverne and Shirley were the comedies that drew our attention during that era.

The radio was always on during the mornings when we lived at the Circle M. Mother listened to country and always had to catch the news. The only song I remember being fun was "On top of Spaghetti." After we moved to Center, I don't ever remember it being on, although it sat on Mother and Daddy's headboard in their bedroom. As a teen, I tried to have the radio on in my room at night, but music is a compelling distraction to doing homework for me. I would start out doing math and be singing along to the music in a matter of a couple of minutes. Two hours later, I would be on the same math problem, but I sang along with 20 of the top 40 during that time. I still cannot carry on a conversation if the TV or radio is on. My brain automatically goes to that medium instead of focusing on the people in the room.

As a young child, our shopping was limited. The grocery store was Libby's in Tenaha, and if we needed clothing- which seemed quite rare, we would go to Carthage, Center, or the Sear's catalog. Cassidy's in Carthage had girls' underwear and socks, Center had shops to accommodate men and boys. Shoes were the only thing we ventured out any farther. Susan wore a EEE width shoe, and the only place that sold children's shoes that wide was at Toy Fair in Shreveport.

When we got older, we would make an occasional trip to Nacogdoches for something, or to eat out at El Pollino's. Lufkin had a catfish restaurant that Daddy liked, and Carthage had the Joe's Grill and Cafe. We never shopped in the large cities like Dallas or Houston. Grandmother and Mother thought they were so big we couldn't find anything.

My first allowance was $0.35/week beginning when I was around 8 years old. I saved forever in order to make my first purchase. I bought a camera for $9.00 from the Sears catalog. It came with little accessories and I could hardly wait for it to come in the mail. By the time I was eight years old, Mother and Daddy had allowed me to open my own savings account at the Citizens Bank in Tenaha. I remember making deposits, sometimes as small as $2.50 and sometimes as large as $50.00 if I sold one of Barbara's colts at the sale barn. I always deposited the Christmas $5.00 from Grandmother and Grandaddy Hancock because I knew he would ask about it the very next week. "What did you do with your money, Cheryl?" was a predictable question the week after Christmas every year for Grandaddy. Mother and Daddy had each one of us kids a separate savings account in Center. For each birthday, they deposited $5.00 multiplied by the age you were that year. They did that for each one of us until we began college and then it was to be used for school.

When we were kids, Cokes cost $0.25 and a candy bar was $0.10. A trip to the country store, Ned Dean's Grocery, on Hwy 59 between Tenaha and Carthage at Woods Community was a treat. In summer, we were huge fans of the fudgecicle, but the rest of the year, a Zero bar was my favorite. We always made a trip during the times we were cleaning out chicken houses- after we worked all day. It was the reward for sticking to a long, hot, and stinky job that had to be done.

As a kid, I never hired out as a babysitter. I had brothers and sisters already. Why would I intentionally want to watch others? I did babysit once for a family on the Tenaha Hwy as a teen. The parents came back later than agreed on, and the father had been drinking and wanted to drive me home. Forget that. I called Daddy to come get me and that was the end of babysitting for others.

My first real job was that of a "soda jerk." I worked for Mrs. Gary in the soda fountain in the Medical Arts Pharmacy drugstore beside the First National Bank in Center on the square when I was 13 on Saturdays. She paid me a $20.00 bill for working from 7:00AM-5:30PM. I stood up all day with a lunch break sometime after 2PM, and one bathroom break. I learned how to make sodas, milkshakes, cherry Cokes and Dr. Pepper's, and hamburgers and cheeseburgers. I learned the waitress shorthand, and how to bus tables and wash dishes in a setting other than home. I also learned this was not the job I wanted for the rest of my life.

19. Doctors and Dentists

The doctor we used was Dr. Grundy Cooper in Carthage until we moved to Center and then we all used Daddy's doctors, Dr. Oates, Sr. and his son, Dr. Steve. Dr. Oates, Sr. was a character. He invented a creosote throat swab for severe cases of sore throat and strep. It tasted awful, just like creosote, but helped immediately. He also invented the creosote shot. It was administered in the hip and he always asked when we could taste it. Within seconds after we got the shot, it tasted awful on our tongue!!! It always brought a chuckle from Dr. Oates. On occasion, we did return to Carthage. When Richard and I got married, I used Dr. Cooper for my pre-marital appointment. I did not want everyone in Center knowing about my life as a married woman. Of course, when I got to Carthage and Dr. Cooper and I were talking about our options on birth control, he said the only sure method of birth control was a dime between the knees. I could have died!

Our dentist was Dr. Rodgers in Center. The older Dr. Rodgers was always a treat, as he did a magic trick every time he had to fill a tooth. With the leftover silver, he always made a brand new nickel for me! I hated going to the dentist, but at least this was some kind of retribution. His office was upstairs above a drug store on the East side of the square so when we came down, we could always stop at the drug store. His son became our dentist after the older Dr. Rodgers died. He is still the one that knows how to handle the way my nerves run in my mouth, and knows that there are times my mouth will not deaden to work on it.

20. Vacations

Mother loved vacations. I never heard Daddy talk of taking vacations as a child, or Mother either, for that matter. But they made sure that our family took vacations. Even before Dave Ramsey and the envelope system, Mother designated the batch of chickens that came off in late May as vacation money. It probably could have been spent more sensibly on school clothes, additional groceries, etc. but Mother wanted our family to see as much of the United States as possible. The only problem we had was that after we saw the Rocky Mountains that was the direction we always wanted to travel. When I was two, Mother and Daddy took Aunt Sally with us and explored West Texas, some of New Mexico, and Arizona. When I was six, Mother and Daddy decided that Gloria and Virginia, my cousin and her best friend that were graduating that year, would be given the opportunity to go with us to Yellowstone. A lot of the families in our community never did travel, so that was a HUGE graduation gift. Mother wanted to invest in those two- they served as our pianist and organist at our church at Woods since they were early in high school.

That trip was an adventure! Mother and Daddy were supposed to pick me up from the last day of school but stopped the bus at the natural gas plant just out of Carthage because they were running late. We had our suitcase packed and Susan and I were allowed to take a tiny little suitcase with our crayons, color books, and a couple of toys. We also were allowed to buy a souvenir or two along the way- hence the acquisition of my blue water gun. We traveled by car- a light brown Chevrolet with wings. It was an early 1960's model. Susan sat between Mother and Daddy in the front, and I was between Virginia and Gloria in the back. Our crayons melted because we stored them on the back dash and the sun was intense, and there was no AC in the cars then. Virginia and Gloria had never been out of Panola county- so everything was new to them. Mother got a chuckle from Virginia when she didn't know how to order eggs- she wanted them like her mother cooked them. Neither had anticipated what we would find in Yellowstone. Of course, Mother and Daddy hadn't bargained for some things either. We drove into Yellowstone with snow everywhere!!! It was 6-8 foot deep where the snowplows had cut through, the bears were everywhere- mama bears with two or three cubs each, moose and elk, and buffalo around the thermal pools. That didn't include the incredible "post card" pictures of snow hanging on fir and cedar, or the magnificent waterfalls, mud pots, and geysers! We had all packed shorts- no pants, no sweaters, and no coats, for sure! When we left home it was 90 degrees! I remember getting out, playing until we froze, climbing back into the car, getting warm and getting out and doing it again. We were gone for two weeks, saw so many interesting things, and were ready to go again! Incredible!

When I was in Jr. High, Mother and Daddy bought a 16 foot travel trailer. Seven people trying to sleep in 16 feet. Now that was fun!! We were packed like sardines, but we all loved to travel, so we just accepted it and enjoyed it. As long as we were cool, we could sleep anywhere.

Over the years, we discovered our perfect weekend get-a-way at Petit Jean. We started out staying at the lodge, advanced to the RV park when we began to pull a travel trailer, and then stayed in the duplexes as we got older. We tried to make a trip there every fall or spring, and it seemed to pacify the longing for the mountains when we couldn't get away for a long trip.

Another much anticipated short get-a-way trip was Blanco State Park below Austin. We traveled there often. The campground sat on a knoll just across the river. All of us kids thought it was neat to see there was no bridge over the river. In fact, the road dipped and the river flowed over the road. We drove through the river in order to cross. The interesting thing about Blanco was that it served as a hub for day trips. We could visit LBJ ranch, drive into Austin or numerous other locations, explore, and come back to the campgrounds at night. We loved the grilling and cooking out over the fire, and the low stress vacationing. Blanco was the site of my very first river float.

On one trip, we went to Robstown, below Corpus Christi. Bro. Thompson had moved there and we went to see them. John was a baby. We went to the beach and picked up seashells and ate our first authentic Mexican food of tamales from a roadside vender. It was at the end of that vacation that we received the call that either Uncle Emory or Aunt Martha had died, and we drove from Corpus to Dallas.

In 1968, Grandmother, Mother, Aunt Rosa Lee, Susan, and I made a trip to San Antonio for the world's fair. The Hemisfair was set to run in Texas, and they decided it would be the closest one we would ever see, so they took us. I remember so many nationalities represented, and I had purchased a notepad to scribble notes on before I went. I asked people from all different countries to write the words, "Jesus Christ" in their native language in it, and that was my souvenir from the trip. Susan wanted a huge tissue paper flower, so Aunt Rosa Lee bribed her by telling her if she was good all day, she would buy it for her before we left. Susan remembers shutting her mouth, and walking away with the flower at the end of the day!

One year we went east and checked out the Smoky Mountains, played at Gatlinburg and rafted down the river. That introduced us to the rafting that our own kids seem to enjoy while vacationing. It was really pretty, but I was disappointed as I thought the mountains would be jagged and majestic like the Rockies. To this day, I still prefer the mountains in the West over the ones in the East.

Regardless, we always vacationed in June from the assets that Mother provided by raising that batch of chickens. She always stressed how much one could learn by traveling that a textbook might not, and sometimes cannot teach. We could name states and locations, and the crops grown in the different states. We knew where the mountains were, the animals that lived in different areas, some of the different cultural aspects, etc. She also knew that once we saw certain things, we understood- and would remember things that would be forgotten by simply reading a book. I doubt she ever fully realized the impact traveling had on the five of us- we all love to see different things, experience different places, and have a desire to see more than we already have! I bet Mother wouldn't have believed that her oldest has traveled to Europe and into the Middle East by herself.

21. Discipline

My Mother and Daddy grew up knowing what it was like to experience the switch when they misbehaved. I never experienced the switch, although two sides of our yard at the Circle M had hedge as a border inside the fence. Mother had a belt that hung on the doorstop attached to the bar that separated the kitchen from the living room. It kept the door from hitting the bar, and was the perfect height to hang the belt. If I needed it, she would fold it in half, and apply to the bottom. It never was applied to my legs, back, or thighs, but strictly on the rear. We never had to lie across the bed, or strip to the underwear; we just learned to dance during the application. I don't remember knowing that they had to stop at three licks like kids think today, but it was never very excessive. It definitely did make a mental impact, however. I remember Grandmother keeping us one year as Mother and Daddy were attending night classes at Panola. Occasionally she would have to threaten us, but I don't ever remember her actually having to spank me. I ran from Mother one time. She stood at the door and very calmly said, "Just remember that you have to come back into this house eventually. It is going to be 10 times worse when you run." That was the only time I pulled that one. When I was in Elementary one summer, we went to Pike's Peak. It must have been a long trip for Mother and Daddy because when we got to the top of the mountain, Daddy found a wooden paddle in the gift shop and bought it. From then on, the belt was retired, and if we needed a spanking, it was from Daddy, and with the board.

My last spanking was when I was 17. We were planning Mother and Daddy's 25th wedding anniversary celebration. I left school that afternoon and stopped at the flower shop on the way home to order the flowers for the renewal of vows we were planning. I had been given instructions to go straight to school and straight home. Of course, Daddy came by the flower shop, saw the car, and questioned me when he got home. I was sassy with the reply, "You know Daddy, you don't have to know everything that goes on in this family." It earned me a meeting with the board.

There were several forbidden areas in discipline. We children knew that sassing was always punishable by the belt or board. We knew never to backtalk. We never hit or slapped Mother or Daddy, and they never hit or slapped us as well. (Regardless of the modern argument about hitting and spanking, *we knew* the difference, and *we knew* when we deserved the spanking.) We never cursed our parents- in fact cursing was never acceptable in our language- period. Lying was punishable by belt or board and was a particular pet peeve of both our parents. I don't know what the punishment for stealing would have been. Susan and I never crossed that line. Joyce found the jars and coin books that Mother and Daddy had with the coins they were collecting, and used it for extra snack money while she was in school. I don't remember what punishment was for her, I just remember Mother telling me about it.

Most of the time, Mother and Daddy would talk to us, paddling or spanking was used as a last resort. Both of them were very good in stating the guidelines beforehand, so we knew our perimeters of behavior. From what I can remember, we minded pretty well most of the time.

22. Chores

Chores were just something we did growing up. We helped fold washcloths even before we were big enough to fold towels. I cooked breakfast for Susan and me while standing in a chair at the stove long before I started school. It was a gas stove, and Mother showed me how to light the pilot light if the burner refused to light when I was a young child. I was scrambling eggs for Susan and me by standing in the chair. As a child, I remember hanging clothes on the line, bringing them in when they were dry, and folding while we sat on the couch. Susan and I both would have chairs at the sink while we were washing and drying dishes. We sat the table, we cleaned our room, we fed the dog and cat, and went with Mother to feed the chickens and take care of the cows and horse. Occasionally when we had pigs, we helped with that as well. The dog and cat, and the rabbits when we were older, were the only ones we were responsible for taking care of ourselves. The others we helped Mother or Daddy. We helped in the garden pick, plant, etc. Those were family chores and we all helped.

After we moved to Center, Mother and Daddy would assign the cooking on occasion to the girls. We all had our specialty. We still folded clothes- in fact, one of the largest arguments Susan and Mother had was over the correct way to fold a towel. Mother wanted them all folded in fourths, with the corner at the upper right-hand corner. Susan just wanted them folded, so there were quite a few that required the refolding under Mother's supervision. After the pool was built, I was the one to vacuum the backyard pool. John or Alan vacuumed the big pool after it came to be, but it was a lot harder to vacuum than the little pool, I was grateful that the boys inherited that chore. I also mowed the yard after we moved to Center and we bought our first riding mower. I loved it- and still do!! The reward is immediate and it gives me time to think without being interrupted. Before I graduated, Daddy began to pay us for mowing. We thought it was great to get $5.00 for mowing an acre and it taking four hours while avoiding the azaleas, and not turning the mower over on the embankment at the end of the house!! In the fall we would rake leaves- an ALL day job in order to get the treat of a chocolate milkshake from the DQ. We were so easily enticed!

23. Not an Only Child

When Mother discovered that she could not have any more children, she became extremely depressed. Sometimes depression can cause people to make decisions that are not as rational as they should be. She deeply longed for other children. She hunted through many adoption agencies and was turned down because of the lack of a separate bedroom for the perspective child, or because we did not meet certain financial requirements. At one point in time, she told Daddy she was ready to go black market for a child. That was not the route God had planned, but it always seems the darkest right before the dawn. God's plan was evident shortly thereafter. Somehow Mother had gotten information about a doctor in Shreveport that was caring for a mother that intended to give a child up for adoption. On Christmas Eve the year I was three, a lady drove up to our house, brought a baby into our living room wrapped in a blanket, and Mother began to wipe the tears. Daddy could hardly contain himself, and they both were explaining to me at the same time that this was my new baby sister. She was ours! As a three year old, my thought was, "If this is our baby, then why doesn't that lady hand the baby to Mother?" She eventually did and it turned out to be the absolute best Christmas ever! Susan had made it to our house. She was six months old, straight blonde hair, little short feet, and the sweetest smile you've ever seen! As soon as the case worker left, Mother called Grandmother and Grandaddy and they were there in just a matter of minutes, as well as Uncle Charles, Aunt June, and their kids. I was told that Mother and Daddy frantically had to buy supplies...and Christmas ...for a new little one. That night we went to Grandmother McDaniel's for Christmas Eve supper as usual, and the whole family couldn't believe it!

A couple of years later Mother and Daddy began to take the steps to adopt another child. This time, they found a door open through the Homes of Saint Mark in Houston. Truthfully, a small two bedroom house can get to be too small for a growing family. They proceeded anyway, and when the wheels of progress moved ever so slowly, they were patient. They were approved, even with his baby bed in the room with Mother and Daddy- and nowhere for a bed to fit after he outgrew the baby bed. At one point, Daddy came home and told Mother to get the bottles out and get things ready. He just had a feeling they were about to get a phone call. Sure enough, John was born on Sept. 23, 1963, and we got the call to come pick him up when he was about a week old. He was another little blonde-headed child, Daddy's first boy! We all remember John making sounds that we hadn't even thought of. He knew how to make the car sound while playing without anyone showing him. He was rough and tough, 100% little boy, and Mother loved to dress him in little overalls as a baby and toddler. When he was a baby, his stomach valve was not working as it should, and he wound up in the hospital when he could not keep any of his formula down. Mother walked the floor with a little crying baby because she couldn't bear to make the sweet little woman that shared the hospital room listen to John cry. We thought it a rare tidbit of information when we found that she was Jim Reeve's mother that shared a room with John as an infant. He finally got to holding down a tiny bit of formula after two weeks in the hospital and did not have to have surgery after all.

After we moved to Center and bought the house on the Logansport highway, Mother and Daddy began the process to adopt Joyce. This time the house was big enough and Daddy's salary had increased substantially. Once again, Daddy came home in November and told Mother he had the feeling they were about to get a phone call. She got things ready, but no phone call. January rolled around and the phone call finally came. When we got to Houston to pick her up, the case worker explained that she was two months old and had been born with a kidney infection. While Mother was holding her, the case worker explained also that if we got her home and it flared up again and we couldn't keep her or didn't want to keep her, we could bring her back. Mother just about flipped. When they handed her the baby, Joyce was ours. There was no way that baby was going back! Mother just was beside herself- the very idea- if she had birthed that baby, she wouldn't be going back! There was nothing that was going to change that Joyce belonged in our family.

When I was 13, our family adopted Alan. Another little blonde-headed boy joined the family- with the adoption process being smooth. At that point, this was the third child from Homes of Saint Mark, so the whole procedure was a little easier. In fact, when Daddy got the "feeling," Mother got things together and within a week the phone call came in and we picked up Alan when he was two days old. I remember the case worker taking us down to a lower floor at the adoption agency in a holding room. Mother and Daddy had to wait upstairs. She went across the street to the hospital, brought the baby back, and we kids got to meet Alan and hold him first. That is a powerful impression in making sure the adoption is a family decision and the baby is accepted! We all thought it was extra special to have seen him before Mother and Daddy did. Alan was such a happy baby. He smiled all the time, except for his first year in swim lessons when he didn't want his eyes to get wet!!!

I guess I thought my brothers and sisters were extra special. Adoption was a deliberate family action that was preceded by prayer from all of us. I remember little things about Susan when we were little. She loved to come up to me from behind and hug my neck. I used to color in the hall under the attic fan and never could finish a picture without her hugs. When she got old enough to color, I remember she always worked with her tongue sticking out. I remember she was sensitive and would cry easily, and she was always where I was. As we got older, we played well together, with just an occasional fuss. We had precious few fights, but the one I do remember was as a teen, when she tied into me at the end of the long hall in the house on Hwy 7. I was wearing a blouse and skirt. By the time we got to the other end of the hall, she had torn the skirt completely off of me, and the blouse was torn as well. I vowed at that time to never provoke her to that level again. We could have verbal fights- but never the hitting, pinching, fist swinging cat-fights again!

When John came along, he played like a typical boy. He was loud and he was always in the dirt, loved fishing, shooting guns, etc. My favorite memory as teens was one night we were listening to Daddy's scanner and we were listening to the police chasing an escapee along Hwy 7 coming from Nacogdoches toward Logansport. He was driving a small white car and then it went silent. We didn't hear anything else on the scanner. Daddy was out working a wreck, and Mother locked the house. We then noticed that there was a small white car parked across the road at the big pool. John and I got two guns, loaded them, went out the back door, and commando crawled around the back yard pool and up beside the fence until we could get to the car and inspect it. Mother was a basket case inside, and when we got back, we were giggling so hard, we made her mad. Needless to say, it wasn't his car.

  Joyce was the talker of all of us. When she was two, Mother would sit her on the bar, give her a spoon and a bowl of cookie dough to stir, and when we got off the school bus, she would have us cookies baked. Joyce always had to have things proven to her. She never seemed to want to listen to reason. She had to experience something to decide if it was bad or good. She was such a live wire as a little girl, and I always wanted her to come visit after Richard and I got married. Things were never dull with her around.

  I remember Alan as a kid just being glad to be with people. He was always smiling and loved socializing with anyone that would pay him any attention. He still does that to this day, and the only times I saw him cry was when he was five and in his first swim class, and the day I had to tell him that Daddy had died.

  After we moved to Hwy 7 John and Alan spent a lot of time playing at the creek that ran behind our house. They would shoot snakes, catch frogs, crayfish, pick berries, etc. I don't know just how far they explored, but the majority of the time they stayed within earshot of Mother or Daddy hollering for them to come in.

  When I got grown and had Robin and Dustin, Alan got a go-cart. I would be right in the middle of teaching swimming and catch a glimpse of Alan with one of my babies coming down the hill just a scooting. I'd think, "He is going to kill one of them before I can get out there." Then I'd look over the fence and see John taking one of my babies off the high dive and they would be just giggling. I *knew* they were going to kill them!

One summer when I went in, John had purchased a motorcycle. I was determined to learn to drive the thing, so he took me in baby steps and I could get it into second gear before swim lessons was over that year. At least I could get it fast enough to make it to the top of the hill and back. That was on my bucket list for the longest...but it just doesn't hold the luster it used to.

24. Our Social Fun

Our social events as a child all revolved around family and church. We met with Grandmother and Grandaddy Hancock's family the Sunday lunch before Christmas, when Uncle Emory and Aunt Martha or Aunt Pauline and Uncle Jens came down from Lancaster, for Grandmother or Granddaddy's birthday, and special occasions. We were always over there it seemed on regular days. Grandaddy always made a round to see us daily- most of the time before Mother went to the chicken house while she was cooking us breakfast. He wouldn't stay long- but just checking in before he went to check on Uncle Charles as well. Most of the time, we made a pass to their house either around lunch or before Daddy got home at 5:30. If it was at lunch, of course we ate, and thought that was the norm as well. I don't know how Grandmother managed to cook without knowing who or how many were going to show up.

Grandmother McDaniel's house was a little more planned. We would be there for birthdays, Christmas Eve, and if a special invitation was given. We didn't pop in with quite the freedom like we did for Mother's family. Of course as a small child, they still owned and operated the Shamrock Cafe in Tenaha so they were at work a lot of the time. We did occasionally spend a Saturday or Sunday afternoon at Mackie and Aunt Sally's house as well. They basically raised Daddy so he was especially close to his Grandmother and Aunt. Mackie really liked Mother. Since Mother never felt really accepted by Grandmother

McDaniel, the fact that Mackie did was well noted. In fact, on one of Mackie's birthdays, Mother baked her a cake and we loaded into the car to make a visit with birthday cake situated in the floorboard of the car. It made the trip just fine, but as we climbed out, John's foot landed right in the middle of Mackie's cake. Mother was greatly embarrassed when she walked into the house with the cake and a two-year old's footprint right in the middle. Mackie looked at the cake and chuckled softly under her breath. Her words were priceless. She looked at Mother and said, "Aren't we glad we have that little boy to make footprints, Bobbie Jean!" She knew how very much Mother wanted a large family. And that was one reason Mother loved Mackie.

25. Cousins

I was fortunate to have a first cousin on the McDaniel side that was two weeks younger than me. Anytime we could persuade Mother and Aunt Vaudrine, we were together. It just wasn't often enough. Aunt Vaudrine introduced me to fried grits and the perks of living close enough to walk to a store to buy a Coke and candy bar. Uncle Jimmy was always a kidder, and I enjoyed the times I spent at their house- whether for the afternoon or to spend the night.

One the Hancock side, I had Kay that was nine months older than me. Nettie was two years older than I was, and Alice and Shirley were older than that. The older cousins were always kind to me and allowed me to hang around whatever they were doing at the time. Summers were always anticipated as I would get to spend a week in Lancaster with Kay as a youngster, and then she would spend a week with me in Tenaha. She would entertain by taking me skating and swimming. I always thought it intriguing that they kept Snickers in the refrigerator- available at anytime. When she came to my house, she had to adjust to no air conditioning. I know it was rough on her. We entertained by riding horses, riding the axle on the trailor back and forth like a seesaw, playing an occasional board game, and taking walks to the ponds. I know it was slightly less entertaining than what they had for me. Once they moved to Tenaha, we tried for more sleepovers- which consisted of Snickers, the Beatles or Monkey's albums, and all night Monopoly games. Those can last forever!

When Kay was in Lancaster, my companions were Nettie, Alice, and Shirley. They would ride horses and I could ride along on Flash. We rode all over their 400 acres, our 169 acres, and sometimes we rode the mile to Granddaddy's. I watched them chase rabbits, played hide and seek or chase around the house with them, and hung around during their chores of washing clothes or working in the garden. They attended all of my little birthday gatherings, and I remember that they always had the most beautiful dolls that sat on their dressers. The dolls Susan and I had were drug through the dirt, half naked most of the time, and their hair (if they had any when Susan got through with them) was always a mess. I really idolized my cousins in so many ways they probably never knew.

26. The Shamrock Cafe

Grandmother and Grandaddy McDaniel owned and ran the Shamrock in Tenaha. It started out as a carhop with the girls riding their roller skates to take the orders to the cars. The light yellow ocher brick building with the rounded end windows trimmed in green was the hub of activity for many years in Tenaha. By the time I came along, it was a sit-down restaurant. Inside were booths along the right and left front windows and along both sides. On the right side there was room for tables as well. On the left side was the counter with red swivel bar stools where most of the men would sit. Immediately when you walked in was the end of the counter with the ice cream box and cash register. Behind it was the window for order pickup. On top of the counter above the ice cream box was the Lance racks that held the round packages of peanut butter and cheese crackers. At the far left sat the Jukebox, and selectors sat on all the booth tables.

We ate many Sunday lunches at the Shamrock, as well as many vanilla ice cream cones. It was here that I learned a little about ordering as a kid. I remember ordering chicken fried steak, cut the steak. My Daddy just stared at me. I knew by his look that I had done something really dumb...but I didn't know my statement meant I didn't *want* the steak. I thought I could ask them to cut it up in the kitchen for me! Everyone's favorite meal was a chicken fried steak- pounded real round steak with thick white gravy!! I also remember that the first shrimp I ever ate was after the Shamrock shut down and Daddy brought two bags that were in the cafe freezer home for us to cook.

Grandmother worked hard and did a little bit of it all. She always had her apron on and her package of cigarettes in the pocket along with her order pad. She waited tables and took orders, cooked as needed, and bused tables. Grandaddy would cook, and do books- but I don't remember him waiting tables. He and Grandmother both poured coffee, and seemingly had as much as they poured for their customers, too!!

Grandmother always had intermittent periods of time that her drinking interfered with the running of the cafe. On occasion, Grandaddy did also. The year that Grandaddy was in the TB hospital was especially hard on Grandmother, and was probably the year that sealed the fate for the Shamrock, and it shut down. It was always such a sad thing to see Daddy get called to come get Grandmother from a business in town, or from the cafe, and to take her home. She would talk ugly, cry, and fight him. He would load her into the car with her fighting him, bring her home, find her stash and empty it, and put her to bed. I have never seen the hurt in my Daddy's eyes as much as when he had to take care of his drunken mother. It was those times that I swore I would never drink, or allow it to be present in our home if I could help it. I have yet to see *anything* good that comes from drinking.

27. The Influence of Church

We grew up in New Hope Woods Baptist Church. My earliest memories of church were sitting on the second row on the right side beside Grandmother Hancock. She would draw stick people bodies, and then my job was to add all the pieces- the hair, eyes, fingers, toes, clothes, hair bows, etc. Mother and Daddy sat right behind us so if I got wiggly, Mother or Daddy would lean up and it would take care of the matter. Mother always made sure we were dressed for church. Between Grandmother Hancock sewing matching dresses for Susan and me, and Mother doing the same, and adding the little white gloves, patent leather shoes, and purse, we were decked out when we went to church- complete with those scratchy petticoats little girls had to wear. Susan would walk in, and before she would sit down on the pew, she would flip up her dress and petticoat on the back side so she wouldn't be sitting on it on the seat. When I visit that church today, Mrs. Birdie Kyle still reminds me of that and still laughs as she recalls watching Susan make her entrance.

Grandmother taught the Beginner Sunday School class. I remember the huge pictures for the lessons and her teaching me the Bible stories. She taught us the little songs like "Jesus Loves the Little Children", "Deep and Wide," and "Jesus loves me." I don't remember her voice as she sang- but the words stuck. I can still see some of the pictures that were used- the multitude sitting on the hillside as Jesus taught, the little boy with the fish and loaves, etc. They also had neat toys after the lesson and the color page we had of the story that we could color. And it was in that class that I was introduced to play dough and finger painting. We never had it at home. Most importantly, she was the one that made the Bible stories come to life. I wanted that for my children, and I want that for my grandchildren. I want the Bible to be alive...for it to be the unquestionable truth that they have known all of their lives.

Grandaddy and Grandmother never sat together in church. Grandmother held down the second pew from the front on the right side of the church, but close to the center aisle. Grandaddy always sat with Mr. Jep Kyle on the third pew near the outside close to the Jr. Sunday School class. It was probably a good thing. Each and every Sunday Grandaddy would take a little nap between the reading of the scripture and the invitation. One day while Bro. Crowell was pastor, he asked Grandaddy why he always went to sleep. Grandaddy's reply went something like this, "Well, I always make it through the singing and the scripture reading and then I let you get started. If it looks like you can handle it, I just turn it over to you and let you have it."

Daddy and Mother worked with the youth and young people- high school and college age. They were good at it because even before it was widely known and publicized in the Baptist church, they worked at the relationship piece of growing a Christian, and the young people loved them. We had Halloween carnivals in our back yard where Daddy built booths- 5-7 booths and he did a fully decked out spook house in the storage room that took weeks to put together. We had hay jumping contests, wiener roasts with Yoo-hoo chocolate colas, and volleyball games. We had Christmas hayrides to go caroling, they organized visits to different homes, and I remember the best hot chocolate I ever drank was in a little house that couldn't hold all the youth that came. It was a cold, uninsulated little house with very meager belongings, where an older couple lived, but they opened their small house to the youth. That makes an impression, even on a little kid that was just there because Mother and Daddy worked with teens, and there was nowhere else for me to be.

  Bro. Thompson was our pastor at Woods Post Office (the church was New Hope Woods Baptist Church and the community was Woods Post Office) during my very young years. He and his wife loved and nurtured Mother and Daddy in their Christian walk. Mother became a Christian when she was 19. She married Daddy at 19 and he was not a Christian at the time. During the years that they lived with Grandmother and Grandaddy Hancock, Daddy witnessed what being a Christian is really all about. He saw that they were real people, had real problems, but their way of handling their life decisions involved prayer, Bible reading, church services, and walking by faith... marching to a different drummer than the world. During that time, he became a Christian. I watched my Mother and Daddy grow in their walk with the Lord after I was old enough to pay attention to these things. He became a deacon and when I was 12, Daddy surrendered to preach. We had family meeting immediately. I knew he was struggling with some decision- he was grouchy, withdrawn, stressed, and would disappear to the big pond for alone time. When he sat us down and told us what was going on, I was shocked. When he told Grandaddy Hancock, Grandaddy cried and he shared something that was very private. God had called him to preach years earlier but he did not answer the call. I had never seen my Grandaddy cry, and I knew what was happening at our house was bigger than big.

Then Daddy shared what he felt our family was about to face, and what example we were to be for others. It included setting a higher standard for our family. It meant giving up a few things that others might find a stumbling block-all shorts for us, and it included smoking for him. It also meant we added some things to grow and strengthen us- including *daily* Bible readings for the whole family. It was a definite change. Then I realized something that rocked my world. This church that had been our stronghold of love, social events, spiritual growth, etc. was not going to be our church home much longer. As a pastor, we would go where Daddy would pastor. But God even let that transition be one that was easier than it could have been. Daddy's first church to pastor was Hawthorne Baptist at San Augustine. They had such a small congregation (6-15) that they only met twice a month. That allowed us to be at Woods twice a month as well. I think that during this time with such a small group is where he coined the term for himself as a "corn patch preacher." Eventually, he became the pastor of East Center Baptist Mission, a mission church from First Baptist in Center. They had no pastor, no song leader, no pianist, and no Sunday School teachers. Daddy preached, Joyce led the music, I played the piano, and Mother taught Sunday School. Daddy taught Training Union at night. We averaged 15-20 on weekly services when we started and grew to a consistent 35, but if we had a social or VBS, we could have 80-100 present. It was simply amazing. At the point that he took the mission, I had had only a couple of years of piano. It was just enough for me to be introduced to the Baptist Hymnal and I could play two hymns. One was "What a Friend We Have in Jesus," and the second was "Nothing but the Blood." For several Sundays, we had to sing the same songs over and over simply because those were the only two I could play. Mrs. Chadwick from Carthage was my piano teacher at the time, and she had just showed me the octave/chord method of playing the left hand. Fortunately, it was the method that most church pianists used at the time and it proved to be the shortcut needed for my learning of hymns, and within about 6 weeks, I was playing more than I thought I possibly could. Necessity sometimes is the best teacher. I remember when one summer approached, VBS was the main event planned. I was the pianist and a teacher. So as an Intermediate, I taught a class of Jrs. In VBS, I must have had 15-18 kids in my class and we didn't have any discipline problems. I am not that good of a teacher, and with only 2-3 years age difference, I doubt that my discipline was outstanding either. I think it was a God thing. The kids were eager, I was stretching for all I could do, and God blessed. This was during a time when revivals lasted two weeks, and if the Holy Spirit was working, the evangelist would cancel his next revival service so he could stay and preach until the Spirit quit moving. I witnessed the decision one night during revival that changed the fate of the Mission. On Saturday night of the first week of revival, the Spirit was moving and people were making decisions. After the service, Daddy, the evangelist, and the song leader, met on the front porch steps to discuss whether to continue the revival the next week or let it end the next morning. The evangelist stated that he really wanted to be in another town the following week, as he did have another revival scheduled. I saw such a defeated look in Daddy's eyes and shortly afterwards, Daddy was called to Patroon Baptist and First Baptist in Center shut the Mission down. I never will forget that sequence of events, and I know that not following the leadership of the Spirit is what shut that church down. It was at Patroon, however, as a 17 year old, I met Richard. That is another story.

I got to enjoy some great Bible basics at Woods. I got to go through Beginner, Primary, and some Jr. Sunday School classes before we left totally for Daddy to pastor. I was introduced to some interesting concepts at a young age. There was one business meeting that seemed to last forever. The "Ten Commandments" movie had just come out and it was going to be showing at the Rio in Center on the square. We discussed at length whether it would be okay to dismiss church and go as a congregation to see it on a Sunday night. At that time, you didn't go to the show, fish, swim, or participate in many "pleasures" on Sunday. There was much debate whether it was ethical to go when we were going to see a Biblically based movie. After the vote, the consensus was to go, and we did, and it was larger than life. When we got home, even I was allowed to stay up really late as we sat at the kitchen table and reread Exodus as a family, just to see if what was shown on the screen was really in the Bible. As a child, it was one of the times I watched my Mother and Daddy proof what the world portrays against the Book. As a youngster, it drove that lesson home. The Bible is the guidebook. It is truth. Everything is to be measured by that standard.

I decided to accept Christ as my personal savior when I was eight. In October of that year I was fully aware that something was missing in my life. There was no peace. I also was very keenly aware that I knew what I needed to do in order to obtain it, but I struggled with the knowledge that I DID understand and where the cut-off would be as one too young to understand. I finally came to the realization that if I did die, I had already had the chance, and ignored it, to make Christ my Lord. One Saturday night I was in Mother and Daddy's room listening to records. One particular song was playing, "Who will take Grandma" by Walter Brennan, the same guy that played Grandpa on the "The Real McCoys." It really got me to thinking that when something happened to me, Jesus would not be there to take care of me because I had already rejected him. I went and got Mother and Daddy and told them it was time for me to accept Christ. I think it caught them totally off guard. They immediately called Bro. Dee Walding that was pastor at Woods at the time and he came and led me in the sinner's prayer and I accepted Christ that night. The next day I remember wishing that the invitation hymn would be "I Surrender All" because that was my favorite invitation hymn...and I wanted it to be "perfect" when I shared with the church the decision I had made. Well, it wasn't "I Surrender All" and I have no clue what it was, it seemed that for a few seconds my feet were made of concrete and couldn't move, and then once I took the first step, I was at the front somehow. I remember being so excited, almost like a weight had been lifted off my shoulders, and wanting everyone to know. Woods didn't have a baptistery at the time, and the next Sunday our whole church went to Tenaha First Baptist for a mid-afternoon baptism service. I also remember standing on the slide on my swing set and telling God that whatever he wanted me to do, I would do. I told him I would be a doctor, a missionary, or whatever for Him someday. I would go to Africa and serve for Him if He wanted, because the only missionaries I had ever heard about served as medical missionaries in Africa. Of course, His plan for me wasn't exactly that. It has been amazing though for Richard and me to be a part of mission teams for several years in the Northwest and Alaska.

When I was 13, I was attending choir at First Baptist in Center along with GA/Acteens on Monday afternoons. The summer following, Mrs. Curtis took the choir to New Mexico on a mission trip. Daddy went along as one of two bus drivers, and I got to go on my first mission trip. We went to the Mescalero Indian Reservation south of Alamogordo, New Mexico. We slept on the pews and floor, and worked for a week helping paint and remodel the church building there. We bought a little swimming pool and put it in the kitchen for bathing- or we could swim in the ice-cold river running parallel with the church building. Typical teens as we were, we established the "pitch someone in the river" routine during lunch each day. Some of us climbed the mountain to the left of the church building every morning before breakfast and petted the horses pastured there. The bathroom was the outhouse, which is pretty scary in the middle of the night with a flashlight and a more than healthy fear of rattlesnakes. We gave a concert the last night there, as well as going and coming to several different congregations. It made such an impact on a young teen as to the needs of people and struggling churches throughout our nation.

Every summer from the time I was old enough to go, I went to Pineywoods for summer church camp. I felt that one day I would love to work camp. At the time I thought it would be as a teenager. I decided I would be a lifeguard there. Little did I know that I would get to work camp, and lifeguard...but it would be in South Dakota, as an adult with a group of college kids on mission trips!!

There have been many times that a simple act of obedience resulted in huge rewards. In May of 1982, Tommy Sparks helped organize the Harletones Senior

Citizen Choir at HBC. At 9:00 that particular morning, Verna Peterson, the pastor's wife, called me and asked what I was doing. I was free, so she said for me to bring Robin to her at 10:00. There was a group at the church that needed a piano player for a new group that was starting. I did, and it began eight years of playing for the most wonderful group of Grandmas and Grandpas there were in Harleton. We would sing at nursing homes from Hughes Springs to Gladewater, Longview, Marshall, Gilmer, and many more in-between. We sang in churches, rode in parades, and anywhere else we were asked to go, we did. Traveling there and back, my kids were nurtured by 25 of the sweetest grandparents God could muster. They loved it, and I deeply appreciated it. After Mother and Daddy were gone, it helped the void that was always lingering. I really think it was a win-win situation. The kids loved the attention, and the Harletones loved having the little ones around. The year that Kalin was born on Dec. 20, we sang in 24 nursing homes between Dec. 1 and Dec. 20. In fact, Dec. 20 was the only day in December that year I had free, so I had prayed specifically that he come on Dec. 20. Each day we left to sing with the Harletones that Christmas, the group prayed that Kalin would not be born that day. God honored that request, and when we got to the hospital on Dec. 20 to be induced, I was just beginning labor on my own. God is so faithful!

28. Early School Days

My formal schooling began in Carthage at age six. There was no kindergarten at that time. I was the last person off bus 18. There was an elderly man, Mr. McDaniel, that drove the bus- no relation- but we got off the bus at 5:00PM in the afternoons and we caught the bus at 6:15AM. I went to Libby Elementary first through third grade and Baker Middle School for 4th and 5th. Laverne Wall was my first grade teacher. Mother just thought she was wonderful, and of course I did, too. Living on the farm, I had never been exposed to the mess of germs that go with a school so I brought everything I could home to share. I had three day measles, red measles, chicken pox, scarlatina, and mono. I don't remember anyone ever mentioning truancy, but I know I must have spent as much time at home as I did at school that year. Mother would make a trip to school, pick up all my school work, and when I returned after an illness, I had to turn every bit of it in. I stayed caught up. I remember my classroom was on the left on the first hall. On the shelves were abacus units, and I had never played with one before. I treasured the days we could pull those out and use them. We began every day with a classroom responsible for the pledge, a devotional, and Bible verse and prayer. We lost a lot of values when we decided that the school was not the place to have an emphasis on God and country. That was also back when we had home visits. I remember Mother being nervous when we had that visit scheduled. I thought it was great fun to ride in the teacher's car home and show her all our great things about living in the country. Mrs. Wall and Mother hit it off and even a couple of years ago at Aunt Rosa Lee's funeral; Mrs. Wall came up to me and visited. What a sweetheart! That was from 1962.

Sometime before my first grade year, I decided that I wanted to be a doctor when I grew up. I didn't want to be a nurse- but a doctor. There weren't many women doctors, so I drew a lot of strange looks at the time. I kept that idea in front of me until I graduated high school and began Panola. And at that time, I realized that I could pursue that as a career and never have the time I knew a family needed, or pursue a career in teaching science and biology and launch the career of others into the medical field. With Richard as a coach, the answer seemed obvious, and I have never regretted the investment in family...or teaching the ones that have become nurses, doctors, physical therapists, etc.

Between my 1st grade and 2nd grade year, Carthage provided free swim lessons for all elementary kids. There had been a drowning the previous year at Lake Murval and the school decided to be proactive in preventing that from happening again. Coach and Nurse Tatum taught the classes. Mrs. Tatum taught the beginners, and after the first year, you paid if you wanted continuing lessons. Of course, Mother thought we definitely needed to continue since we lived around several ponds. I continued through strokes classes with Coach Tatum.

My second grade teacher was Mrs. Murff, my third grade was Mrs. Hudson. It was during that year that I was saved. I wanted the world to know the change that had occurred in my life, and I never will forget what a crusher it was when I told Mrs. Hudson what had happened and her reply was, "That's nice, now run along and play."

Elementary was basically uneventful in the classroom. I could do whatever was asked, but I don't remember being bored to death. I made good grades, stayed on the brink between the top and the second Reading group, and loved all the social interaction with the other kids. One of the treats that I do remember was music class. The music room was right past the principal's office and the little chairs were arranged along three walls in a U. The piano sat at the open end and we learned such neat little songs. I always loved music. My all time favorite from elementary was "Frog Went a Courting."

The other thing that I remember was the pine straw houses and jump rope on the playground behind the school. The big old pine trees dropped straw and we loved to hand rake it up into rows and make the outline of playhouses. We could make a house and spend all of the time making little pine straw furniture, and doorways, kitchens, etc. It was my first experience with house plans, a hobby I still enjoy today. The other thing was the two- man jump rope. "Cinderella dressed in yellow, went upstairs to kiss her fellow, made a mistake and kissed a snake, how many doctors did it take?" Then the rope would go into red hot peppers (super fast) and they would count until you missed- silly little games that were loads of fun for an elementary kid.

In 4th grade we started changing classes, and I had Aunt Rosa Lee for Reading. We had the SRA program. It had Reading cards with questions to answer afterwards. I absolutely hated that reading program. It was boring, they asked stupid questions, and it always tried to trick you. Not only that, I was expected to do good. After all, I was in Aunt Rosa Lee's class and I *had* to do good. At that time, I realized that I might not make all A's in school. It was not my best year!

In fifth grade I had Mrs. Rowe from Old Center as my homeroom teacher. Since we lived between Woods Community and Old Center Community, and it seemed like Carthage was a huge city to this country girl, it was a big deal to actually have a teacher in school that was from the country...and my community as well. I also met one of my dearest friends- Jeannie Hilyard. She and I had everything in common. We could talk endlessly and still need more time to talk. Her father was a pastor too. It was our time talking that earned me my first C in class- in math- because Jeannie and I sat together and visited. Then our worlds crashed. She moved to the Fort Worth area and I moved to Center. We wrote back and forth (way before texting and cell phones), but we didn't get time together after that. A couple of years later, they were coming to church camp at Gary, TX between Carthage and Tenaha and had a car wreck right before they got to the turn off at Gary. Jeannie was killed, and her sister critically injured. We drove to Dallas/Ft. Worth for the funeral. That was the first "best friend" I had ever lost.

Fifth grade also was the beginning of piano lessons for me. I took from Mrs. Chadwick that lived about five blocks behind the middle school. When it got PE time, I would exit, run those five blocks, have a piano lesson, run back to school, and get there shortly after the next class began. I continued to take piano during my 6th grade year in Center under the older Mrs. Searcy. She had a wooden baton and would hit my knuckles when I played the wrong note. I hated it. In fact, I grew to hate piano lessons so much that several times Daddy would drop me off at 7:00 AM for my lesson and as soon as he rounded the corner, I would leave and go to school playing hooky from piano. I told Mother I wouldn't take the following year, and refused to even walk through the living room where the piano stood. She knew I meant it. By the 9th grade year, Mother had found Mrs. Minter, and what a wonderful lady she was. She taught the student to enjoy music- whether you were playing classical, modern, gospel, or just singing along. Our recital that year was in her new house. She had white carpet and the high school girls sat on the floor eating chips and brownies while each one of us took our music (because in real life seldom does a pianist have to play from memory and took turns going to the piano and simply playing our pieces for each other. It was such a relief!! I finally loved it again.

  Sixth grade in school turned out to be a fair year considering that I was not in a school I wanted to be, I hated piano, and I had to make all new friends on top of that. Daddy had gotten a promotion at work to Maintenance Foreman for the Highway Department (TXDOT). It meant a considerable raise, but it meant he must live in the county that he worked. It meant a move away from Grandmother and Grandaddy. It meant moving to the city and Mother hated the city. It meant moving to a rent house. It was bigger, but in worse shape than our house at Woods. Mrs. Fannie Watson was my homeroom teacher and Grandmother Hancock's sister, Evie Moody was my math teacher that year. Mrs. Watson read to us every day right after lunch. I don't know how she did it, but it was magical. She would read softly, and with just the right amount of expression. We would all be totally engrossed in whichever book she was reading. She would limit it to a chapter a day, and we would beg for more. She read <u>Magic Time Machine</u>, <u>Where the Red Fern Grows</u>, <u>My Side of the Mountain</u>, etc. She never raised her voice the entire year. She was and still is one fantastic teacher. We all wanted to stay in her class. No one wanted to leave. She still knows what it takes to entice youngsters to want to learn. Last I heard, she was teaching 6th grade still- but now the GT.

29. Don't Buy Me Any Furniture

Between the 6th and 7th grade, Mother and Daddy bought the house on Hwy 7 on the Logansport Hwy. It was a step up for our family- a four bedroom brick just outside of the city limits. We each got to choose our bedrooms for our furniture. Alan chose the first room down the hall with the silver bookcase headboard furniture for his and John's room. Mother had bought maple twin beds and Grandmother had bought us our sets of sheets when we lived in the rent house, so Susan and Joyce chose those to go in the middle bedroom. Mother and Daddy still had the Western pine bedroom suite from when they got married, so it left me with no furniture in the end bedroom. I told Mother that I really didn't want to go buy anything.

For some reason during that time I had become fascinated with antiques. It wasn't any antique, it was family antiques. I wanted to look around in everyone's barn and see what I could find. Grandmother Hancock was such a help. She took her childhood trunk from when she was a very small child (she was born in 1898) and refinished the inside with red velveteen and recovered the tray with white and gold fleck contact paper. That was such a huge treat- I don't remember her giving gifts to the grandchildren except for the money at Christmas and sewing all of the grandchildren's dresses. Then she gave me the dresser that she and Grandaddy used to begin their marriage. They had paid $15.00 for it- and the price is still on the back of the mirror. She also let me have a set of cotton scales, a model A wrench, a shoe last with 5 shoe molds, the watering jug from the field, and her very last gift from Santa when she was 11 years old (1909)- a pair of inexpensive but beautiful vases that she sat on her bedroom mantle during most of her marriage. (The story is told that she loved flowers from a very young age. She grew them every summer, and would collect bouquets to bring in even as a child. Later, she always grew flowers in her yard, and was responsible for the arrangement each Sunday at New Hope Woods Church during each summer.) She gave me two oil lamps, the lamp that the teachers that boarded in the front bedroom used to grade papers during the time that her own children were growing up, a crock, old pottery milk pitcher, a honey press (called a ricer to most- but she used it to press honeycomb to extract honey, and to mash the yellow from a boiled egg for the top of her potato salad), and two massive framed pictures we found in the bottom of the saltbox in the smokehouse of Grandaddy Hancock's Grandmother and Great-grandmother and Grandaddy taken around 1850. I repainted the frames and they hung in my bedroom. Later I discovered while talking to Aunt Rosa Lee, Uncle Charles, and Aunt Pauline one year at our house here in Harleton during the Hancock Christmas, that Grandaddy Hancock's Great-grandmother was Indian. That explained why his Grandmother had on gold loop earrings in the picture. Otherwise, it was not in line for her to be wearing large earrings, but with Indian heritage, it was a matter of pride to be able to wear such jewelry.

    I never did lose the love of family antiques- and eventually gathered several more family treasures. I acquired Grandmother Hancock's sewing machine that she used to make every dress for the grandchildren. Aunt Pauline made sure I had it before she passed away. When it got time to sell Granddaddy's place, the whole family gathered and drew numbers to see which order we could choose the items in the house. The only piece of furniture I received was the bookcase from the living room. It did contain all the books that remained- which consisted of some of mother's Ag books from school (she was the first girl to be allowed in Ag classes in Carthage). I confiscated a box of trash from the back porch and came home with the measuring spoons and jelly spoons that served as baby toys when we were toddlers, her wire whisk, jelly funnel, the old flatware, her gingerbread pan, some of the ivy dishes we all grew up with, and a glass flower basket with the glass handle wired on.

I was thoroughly surprised when I got home and found four of Grandaddy's ice picks. What a memory! He would order blocks of ice from the Center Ice House and they would be delivered to Grandaddy's house to ice down the drinks for the First Saturday in May cemetery working. He took # 3 tubs, and filled them with bottled drinks, and chipped up the blocks of ice to cover while they were sitting on the back of the old blue farm truck. All of this involved the grandkids "helping" and hanging around- getting in the way I am sure. He would sometimes cover that with a canvas tarp to keep it from melting and then all of us grandkids that were old enough, had the "utmost privilege" of selling those drinks at the cemetery. It was a matter of pride when we could prove to Grandaddy that we could count back money and make change. You got the treat of selling drinks from then on. It was almost like a rite of passage in our eyes.

Everything outside the house on the day that we divided his possessions was just available for whoever wanted them. I gathered old tools from Grandaddy's blacksmith's shop- including an old shovel for ashes, a wooden mallet, a huge wrench, several blades, nuts and bolts, gears, a pitch fork, a whet stone, and a wood planer. When I made the rounds that day, I brought home a turning plow, middle buster, and Georgia stock as well. In the barn loft I found a wooden nest egg- funny how the little things seem such a treasure because they were connected to a childhood memory of gathering the eggs late in the afternoons with Grandmother. Grandaddy had built the nesting boxes on the back side of the stairs going up into the loft. Every day I heard the same warning,"You be sure to look before you put your hand in there. You'll pull out a chicken snake if you don't watch it." I found a chicken house feed scoop, two of my glass baby bottles in the cellar, a couple of glass door knobs in the storage shed, a blue Ball jar, a plow tip, two seed planters with plates for peanuts and watermelons under a shed at the barn, several wrenches, and two plow sweeps, another pitcher, and two spools of thread and a small box of Black Drought from the old store Grandaddy had, too.

  I always thought it was the right thing to do- for us to divide things up before Grandaddy died. I was glad they decided to do it then. I got to visit with Grandaddy several times while he lived with Aunt Pauline his last year, and more than once, I got to tell him thank you for the items I had gotten, why they were special to me and the memories they evoked, and what I was doing with them now. It seemed to please him to know that all of the things that had been a part of his life were not just taken to a landfill, but that the family treasured even the silliest of all possessions- even down to a wooden nest egg.

  I also claimed several pieces that Mother had gathered up and kept, after Mother died. At that point in time, I got Grandmother's Bible, two more of her more modern vases, a gold rimmed sugar bowl, and creamer, butter mold, the colander- which I still use today, the purple tall sugar bowl (from 1865), some of her tatting and embroidery pieces, and the round gold bowl from that time as well. I got Mother's quilt box that Grandaddy had built for her as a child, and I got the beautiful seed picture that hung in Grandmother's living room after Mother died and Grandaddy moved in with Aunt Pauline. Aunt Pauline had taken it to her house when Grandaddy had remarried and she gave it to me after Mother died. Mother had always said that she wanted it, so I guess that was why it was given to me. It was eaten up from weevils, so I spent about 2 months, treating it with insecticide, taking each piece out, repainting, re-doing the background, and putting it all back in. I repainted the frame, and it now hangs in my den. This was originally made by Grandmother Hancock's grandmother and completed in 1900. Since Grandmother said she would visit and she "helped" with it, she either had that as her memory of her grandmother or she was told that from her mother as she got older. It was one of three pictures that her grandmother made- one from seed, one from large buffalo fish scales, and one from human hair that was braided or twisted. As far as I know, the seed picture is the only one that is still in existence. Later on, when Rose Anne sold her house in Sanger, she called me and asked if I wanted Grandaddy's candy counter from the old store. I was elated!! You should have seen Richard's face when we went to pick it up! It was a pile of rubble and he thought the only place it belonged was the dump. We brought it home and this pile of broken glass and wood sat on my front porch until I had the opportunity to get Philip Smith to look at it. He completely put it back together again and delivered it right before Christmas 2009 and it serves as a display/buffet in my dining room.

Later on, when we sold the place in Center after Mother and Daddy died, I claimed the old mantle in the storage room. It had been in Grandaddy's and Grandmother's bedroom from the time their house was built until they remodeled and took out that fireplace, replacing it with a gas heater in the 1950's. Mother had brought it home with her, and I redid it and put it in our bedroom when we built the house. I also claimed the windmill derrick. It is missing the blades, but those are on my list to pick up one trip to West Texas. One year at Christmas, Aunt June and Uncle Charles brought me their butter mold for me to have, too.

While I was hunting furniture for my room as a kid, I also found an iron bedstead at Mackie's house that Aunt Sally let me have. I repainted it, but it came completely apart after Richard and I married. She also let Mother have a glass handle-turned churn that I later acquired, and when they sold Grandmother McDaniel's house in Tenaha, I found a jukebox selector and a milk bottle in the garage. Daddy had found some school books years earlier that his grandmother had used as a child that I have now. When Mother and Daddy died, I claimed Daddy's childhood marbles- I just put them in the blue jar in the candy cabinet to keep them together.

Richard's side of the family kept items that they continued to use. Seldom were things just kept because they were family connected. I did get the well pulley that was from Richard's grandaddy's well (Papa Hardy). We also got a walnut bedroom suite that was made around 1900 in South Texas that was his grandmother's (Granny Hardy). We got Daddy Coot's grandmother's treadle sewing machine and had it redone. I still use the cast iron skillets (one 8 inch and one small) from Mama Joyce that had belonged to Daddy Coot's Mother. I also got crystal stemmed sherbet cups and some plates that belonged to Mama Joyce's family – I think her mother, and a punch bowl with the under plate that belonged to Mama Joyce's mother, Myrtis Williams. We got Daddy Coot's iron bedstead that I have yet to redo.

30. Jr. High and High School

One of the events in the 7th grade was having Mrs. Malone for English. She taught us how to diagram a sentence and that info is invaluable to me even today. I can pick out the parts of speech and mentally picture a diagrammed sentence as I speak. I always felt for Mrs. Malone. I've noticed that no matter what school a student is in, they always seem to hate the English teacher that pushes them. Mother helped me cook lunch for Mrs. Malone at the end of the school year to say thank you for all she had invested in me. She had often talked about how she enjoyed fresh foods from the farm, and that living by herself didn't warrant cooking for herself that often. She was elderly, and I guess she just hit a soft spot in my heart. We surprised her with the meal, and she wrote Mother and me the sweetest thank you note afterwards.

I also had my first stomach ulcer that year. I remember eating broiled meat that entire year, refraining from anything spicy, and wishing this bland diet would help me become skinny. Of course, it didn't work that way. All the girls had a crush on the new science teacher, Mr. Wilkins, and we were one of the first groups that had classes at CH Daniels. It meant that we were bused into the quarters every day.

It was during this time of my life that we decided to learn to sing harmony. Susan and I were totally different in our voices, and both of us were sopranos. Daddy thought I could learn the alto part and then we could participate, instead of just listen, in the Saturday night singings we were attending on a regular basis. Since Aunt Evie and Uncle Jewel traveled and were singing instructors for the Stamps School of Music years earlier, we went to Aunt Evie and I learned the alto part. I can't always hear it in order to sing it however, so it was always a hit and miss. I know that was disappointing to Daddy.

Nothing was eventful during my 8th grade year. My ulcers returned, and I endured. Basically, I did not like my Jr. High years in school, and hoped that High School would be better. When I got to high school, I found that we had three distinct groups of kids- the ropers, the dopers, and the mediocres. The ropers hung out at their pickup trucks between classes, the dopers hung out at the smoking tree at the front of the school, and the mediocres hung out in the halls or the classrooms. I was a mediocre. Aunt Pauline was teaching VOE in a corner room, so I wasn't going to get into much trouble with her watching out after me. I thought it rather convenient for Mother- I have been watched and reported on since I was in the 4th grade from the Aunts in my family. I didn't actually take VOE- as I had absolutely no intention of ever using a business machine or ever working in an office. I did take typing however, and actually was on the typing UIL team back when that existed. I also remember Daddy talking me into playing basketball instead of taking PE. That was a disaster the first year. The very first basketball game I ever watched, I was playing. Makes for some interesting moments...like the girl guarding me as I was throwing the ball from out of bounds just jumping around, waving her arms, and cursing a blue streak at me. I hadn't done anything to her, and I always got along with people, so I lost all concentration on what I was supposed to be doing, and forgot to throw the ball in to a teammate!

The worst thing that happened that year was getting word in November that Grandmother Hancock had died. I think my whole world shook with that news. She had a brain stem aneurism. It had leaked before and somehow against what the doctor had said, recovered. This time she didn't. She had been the rock, the family stability. She had single-handedly taken care of the house, cleaning, washing, cooking, canning, sewing, the gathering of the garden, ...it all. Some pictures seem etched deep within one's memory. The flowers at her funeral were all fall colors of oranges, bronzes, and yellows. Even today when I decorate for fall, there is a memory of Grandmother that floods my senses. It seemed like our family was cut in half with the absence of one. Grandaddy looked so weak without her there. I remember coming to see him after she had died and he was eating cold purple hull peas from the fridge for a meal. They weren't warmed up; they weren't accompanied by cornbread and the various other veggies she always cooked. There was no meat and he was eating all alone. It broke my heart. It wasn't long until he remarried- just out of pure loneliness. Both of his following marriages were disasters. Neither could cook, hear, or knew how to care...just money hungry.

Every year in high school, I would choose something to insure some extra pictures in the yearbook. I guess I was vain. I loved that I could sign the yearbook from one end to the other. Freshman year I won the Betty Crocker award (I never wanted to pursue Home Ec. either. It was just one of those things that came naturally in our family. Everyone learned to cook, to sew, to take care of whatever was needed at the time. We learned a work ethic at all times- not just in a career. If we saw something that needed done, you did it. You did not wait until you were told. I hope we have passed that down to the next generation. Hospitality is bred into the family actions- girls or boys. Who knew that later on I would have six wonderful years as a Home Ec. teacher, too?) I was on the Science UIL team, the Physics UIL team, and continued playing basketball through my Jr. year. Of course, it was the senior year that we went to state in girls' basketball. Bad call on my part to miss out on that. I was in Science club, FHA club, and anything else I could think of. Somewhere during this time, I also took twirling lessons. I never did try out for twirler, but it was fun.

During my sophomore year, I played basketball again, and in off season, began running cross country. At night, Daddy would take me to the airstrip and we would run it for practice. Because the airport had no communications whatsoever, no planes ever landed after dark so we had a paved area with no interference for running. I really did enjoy that part. Coach demanded that all of us girls be in cross country, whether we were on the actual team or not. It was this experience that was responsible for my one and only school paddling. She would take all of us girls to CH Daniels, and turn us loose. We were to run back to the high school before it was time to catch the bus and go home. After about 1 ½ miles, there were a few that began to lag behind. We were running, but a lot slower than when we started. Coach Williams would drive her station wagon up behind the last runner, park her car, get out with her paddle, begin to run after us, and whoever she could catch, got paddled. One day she got me. Mother and Daddy had the policy in place that if any of us kids got a paddling at school, we had two more when we got home. Mother would get us first, and then Daddy would finish it off when he got home. It was well known that they supported the school and the teacher, and they expected us to do whatever was asked of us. I guess for the most part, it was before parents began to take the sides of the child and try everything to get a teacher fired. Right or wrong, we were to respect and follow the directions of the teacher. Needless to say, I didn't advertise that I got a paddling at school- or on the back streets crossing the Logansport Hwy. In fact, I waited until I was grown and been married for about 3-4 years before I admitted at supper one night that I had gotten it in high school...and I made sure Richard was sitting between Mother and Daddy, and me.

    The thing that was worth remembering between my Sophomore and Junior year was the building of the pool in the back yard. Mother and Daddy sold some timber. Since I had just turned 16, they decided to invest in something that would keep me home and bring my friends to our house rather than me hunting something to do elsewhere. Before we got the pool finished, Daddy was already having folks ask if he would teach them or their kids to swim. We literally started teaching swimming before we had all of the deck poured around the pool. Since we were doing it ourselves, we had a portable concrete mixer and it would take an entire Saturday- early until late- to pour an 8 foot by 16 foot section. I started teaching that summer as Daddy's helper. It was that year that a tradition began. I would take orders from Daddy as an employee as long as we were teaching swimming. The last day of swimming, after the last class left, Daddy was going to get pushed into the pool. It was a cure for the frustration caused by biting the tongue for six weeks! It was totally amazing how strong my Daddy was! Before we quit teaching swimming in Center, sometimes we had five instructors that would gang up on him and once he planted his feet, all of us together couldn't get him in the pool. We had to strictly catch him off guard (now that was not easy after he knew it was coming every year) to even have a chance. I guess his years as a young fighter left him with an inner strength and strategy to remain in one spot. Of course, we always had to go eat fish in Lufkin after swimming classes ended each year, too! Of course, Daddy's swim business grew each summer. When I started college, we were teaching three, two-week sessions per summer. They were full- which meant 100 kids/session, or 300 kids/summer. I could go to SFA an entire year on what I made as his helper. I did my Lifesaving at SFA as one of my PE classes and really enjoyed it- even when I had the SFA swim coach, Virginia Matthews, as my partner for the actual test. Daddy then certified me in WSI. Forty-three years later (2015) and I am still teaching swimming during the summer!

    Between my Junior and Senior year, Daddy became the pastor at Patroon Baptist Church below Shelbyville. It was a small church with about 20 people at the time. They did have a song leader- a good looking guy named Richard Hardy. Pat Jones played the piano. My best friend at the time, Sheryl Shidler, lived with us as she just finished her Sr. year and was beginning Panola. She noticed him, too. (This guy disappeared immediately after the last Amen. Literally, I couldn't find him when I got to the door of the church after the service. Later we discovered that he lived directly behind the church.) Daddy's first Sunday to preach there was August 7, 1973.

    I took three college classes my Sr. year. Mr. O'Neal from Panola came to Center and taught History both semesters. Our whole class loved it! He was the only history teacher I have ever had that could bring it to life. I also drove with Mother to Panola one night a week for an Economics class- the most boring of all classes. It was that year that Mother and I also took a cake decorating class- and who knew where that would lead! I was glad to reach graduation. I really felt that I had wasted a year that I needed for college. My high school counselor did not justify, in my eyes, me even being there that year. I only had to get ½ credit that entire year. Speech counted for English and it left me only needing Civics in order to graduate. I was bored...yes, beyond bored! I begged and pleaded to get out early to no avail. The counselor told me that I was not college material and I probably wouldn't go... and she definitely didn't think I would ever finish. Now that I am a lot older, and I can look back, I probably was not a great student. Heaven knows I didn't want to waste an entire year for ½ of a credit... but I did get the college degree, along with a Masters, and a few classes past that. Don't ever tell a kid that they can't achieve a goal, and worse yet, not to try. I just needed to decide what I wanted to do and then given the opportunity to do it. I have thought about getting my Doctorate a few times, but I have to consider that I probably would be getting it solely for spite to rub it in her face...and who knows, she probably has Alzheimer's by now.

Another tidbit of useless information was the Miss Toledo Bend Pageant. I decided, "Why not?" It was just for fun, and several of the girls I knew were going to participate. I played the piano and sang for my talent number, and it was the first time I've ever modeled a swimsuit (coral one piece) and heels in front of a packed auditorium. I didn't win...or even make the top five, but my Daddy made me feel like a queen that night. He had looked at my Mother and asked during the competition,

"Bobbie, what are we going to do if she wins?" It let me know that he thought I was good enough that I could have won. That was enough for me.

Mother and Daddy sent me to Stamps Music School in Murray, Kentucky for graduation. It was the first year they held the school there. Aunt Rosa Lee drove up with us so Mother would have someone else to share the driving. The school lasted for three weeks, and I learned to simply chord a song and add some of the fillers, with a suspended third being the most enticing sound on my ear. It was fun, I learned a lot of different things, met a lot of people, and had my first taste of independence. I took lessons from the Blackwood Brothers and Stamps Quartet. The strangest part of the whole experience was getting mail one day, reading the East Texas Light newspaper from home and Aubrey King from Tenaha walking up wondering who in the world would have a Tenaha newspaper in Kentucky!

After high school, I started Panola. Richard had just finished Panola and began SFA. My first year at Panola was just a continuation of high school. All the teachers knew us by name, and they looked out after us as well. I remember one day skipping English class in order to finish a really good Spades game in the Sub (the recreation hall). I looked up to see my English teacher coming in the door telling me to come on to class. How embarrassing is that for a college student!!!

The next fall I only had three classes I could take at Panola, so I went MWF to Panola and TTh to SFA. At the time, neither college had put that together, so I pulled it off. I do not think we can pull that off today with our modern technology.

31. Daddy's Planes

At this point in time while I was completing high school, Daddy's job allowed Mother and Daddy to begin to breathe a little easier financially. Daddy decided to pursue a life-long dream of flying. He took lessons, got his license, and bought ½ of a small red Piper single engine plane. We loved going up with him. It wasn't long, however, until his partner took the plane to Mexico and wrecked it in the mountains. Mexico never did let that plane come back to the US so Daddy bought ½ of another plane. It was a Cessna twin engine that seated five. Oh this one was great! We would hop in and fly with Daddy to Dallas, or Oklahoma, or wherever. He would let us help fly it; I think to encourage our desire to get our pilot's license as well. He would get up to around 5000 feet and kill the engine and free-fall for about 3000 feet before he would turn the engine back on. That was a thrill! It was also scary! I told him after we had Robin, I couldn't be with him when he did that anymore. Single or even married it was fine, but with a baby to be responsible for, it wasn't happening again. He respected that and we never worried about it again. When he had his heart attack in 79, he lost his license for health reasons, but worked to pass his physical and regained it, and flew until his death in 88. Then we sold his half in the plane to his partner, Bill Watson.

32. Mother and Daddy's 25th Anniversary

Mother and Daddy celebrated their 25th wedding anniversary during the time that Sheryl Jean lived with us. We decided to make it one they would remember. We contacted the preacher that had married them, and he still had the vows he had used in their original ceremony. We ordered a sheet cake and had it decorated in wedding décor, and Sheryl Jean and I made dresses to wear for all of the girls. We told Mother and Daddy we wanted to take them out to eat, but they had no idea they were going to have the family there and they would repeat their vows. I went to the florist and ordered flowers, and Kay was willing to drive the kids over after we ate. Richard and I, Johnny Pollard and Sheryl Jean, and Mother and Daddy met Bro. and Mrs. Thompson to eat, and then went back to their house to visit. She painted as a hobby, so Mother didn't think a thing about a tablecloth covering her table, with things underneath. Soon, Kay showed up with Susan, John, Joyce, Mary Ellen, and Alan. Then Bro. Thompson asked Mother and Daddy to stand up, we handed Mother a bouquet, and pinned a boutonniere on Daddy, and it suddenly hit them what was happening. They were stunned that we had pulled it off. Bro. Thompson led them through the renewing of their vows, and then we sent them on a second honeymoon- complete with nightie! Since I had gotten my last spanking right after I ordered the flowers while we were preparing for this event, I took the opportunity as they were leaving to remind Daddy that I was indeed right...they didn't have to know everything that was going on at our house! He probably should have spanked me again!

33. Dating

I wasn't allowed to date as early as some of my friends. I could have friends that were boys, "boyfriends," that would come to the house, but I was not allowed to go anywhere with any of them until late sixteen. Even then, I had to get it approved by Congress, it seemed. The "Did you ask Mother?" or "Did you ask Daddy?" tactic back and forth repeatedly was the most frustrating tactic ever invented. It turned out to be far easier if the guys just came to the house, and we didn't worry about going somewhere. Going out to eat and seeing a movie was the extent of what was available anyway. I probably had a half of dozen dates before I met Richard.

This is how my interest in Richard unfolded. Daddy went in view of a call to pastor Patroon Baptist in July the year I was seventeen. They had a really cute song leader. He had dark brown hair, worn like Elvis, and he had a sweet little smile. He caught my eye immediately. Daddy accepted the call and his first official Sunday was August 7, 1973. About two weeks later, we had a volleyball game at church, and Richard was on my team. Going for a hit, I fell, and he caught me...! I was totally infatuated! He called a couple of weeks later, and Sheryl Jean and I were both gone. All he said when he talked to Mother was that he had called to talk to Cheryl/Sheryl. We didn't know which one. Then he called again later and asked me out in September. We saw a race car movie that was worse than I wanted to watch, so I left to talk to Wanda working the concession stand. Afterwards, he took me home, gave me a polite kiss, said nothing, and left. It was a total disaster!

He didn't call the next week so I thought that was all of that one. I didn't know that he had to work that weekend. The next week he did call, and we went somewhere- I don't remember the where. What I do remember is what he did after we got home. He parked the car, turned off the motor, and turned to me and said, "I want to talk to you. I need you to know my intentions. I want to get to know you as a friend. If something more develops, that would be great, but I want you to know this. It will be honorable. I will never take advantage of you, mentally or sexually. You don't have to worry about that." Then he *kissed* me. Needless to say he had my attention and I was hooked. No guy had ever leveled with me. When I got in the house and Sheryl Jean asked me how it went, I told her, "I think I am going to marry this guy." That was the greatest kind of romance I'd ever seen! He was telling the truth. He never did take advantage of me. We dated for 2 ½ years and married January 3, 1976. During that time he ate *many* grilled cheese sandwiches, and played *many* games of chess and checkers!

34. Wedding Bells

At the end of September in 1975, Richard and I went to a Shelbyville football game on one of our few "actually leave the house" dates of dating. He took out the box with my engagement ring while we were waiting in the car and he placed it on my finger and I got to go into the stands officially engaged that night. It was neither a surprise nor really romantic- just time. I had helped pick out the ring, we had talked about marriage numerous times, and while he never has really proposed to this day, we just knew it was time. The first folks I got to show my ring to were two ladies from our church, Mrs. Monroe and Mrs. Juanita. When I got home that night, I showed Daddy and his comment was something like, "That's pretty." I woke Mother up and showed her, and she just said, "Uh huh," and then rolled over and went back to sleep.

Richard graduated SFA December 20, 1975. We got married at Patroon Baptist on Saturday, Jan. 3, 1976, at 4:00PM. He had to be back to work Monday night at the Red Barn Steakhouse, so we just had the weekend. We planned a simple wedding. Mother had decided the best way to deal with the presumed fact that I was not going to finish my degree was to ignore what was coming. She didn't speak to me during the months preceding my wedding except to tell me that whatever I wanted to get, remember I was paying for. I was in college and had no job...so pickings were slim. I bought fabric and made my wedding dress for $75.00. I got the cheapest flowers (which were white carnations) and rented an arch at the flower shop and the color was from the ribbons they incorporated. Since Richard wanted a royal blue wedding, the white flowers worked with blue bows. I borrowed ferns from a lady in the church, Mrs. Woodfin, to flank the arch, and my cousin, Linda Sue, made the cake as her gift to us- which was the beginning of her catering and cake career. The guys wore suits, and Mother finally did make the girls dresses from beautiful royal blue velvet trimmed with just a tiny bit of white lace. Since I wanted Daddy to perform the ceremony, I asked Grandaddy Hancock to walk me down the aisle. Richard and I wrote our vows from Daddy's pastor's book of ceremonies and then memorized them. On January 1, Grandaddy had a heart attack. Knowing that the first 72 hours are critical, we didn't know if we would be planning a funeral along with a wedding, canceling a wedding, or what. Plan B came into play. When Linda Sue got to Carthage with the cake, she backed the van up to the side of the hospital, opened the back door, and stacked the cake for Grandaddy to see through his hospital window. My sister, Susan, was my maid of honor, Sheryl Jean Shidler and Pam Johnson were my bridesmaids, and Joyce was my flower girl. Richard's brother, Kenneth, was Richard's best man, Ralph Clark and Kenneth Bohannan were his groomsmen, and Alan was the ring bearer. Pat Jones played the piano. Daddy walked me down the aisle and was crying by the time he got me to the altar. When he turned around and faced the audience, he lost it. Richard and I took over, and said our vows, Carla Christian did the special music, and by then Daddy got it together to do the ring ceremony. Mother never shed a tear. After the reception, we drove to Lufkin, ate at El Chico and spent the next two nights at the Holiday Inn across the road. When we got back to Nacogdoches on Monday, we entered a freshly painted, still wet, apartment and real life began. We promptly went to the grocery store and discovered there is more than one way to buy groceries. His mother bought weekly so the bill was never very high. My mother bought monthly because Daddy got paid once a month, so when she went, it was a complete restocking of the kitchen. With nothing to start with, I assumed we would stock the kitchen. That was not his idea at all...so within 48 hours of getting married, we had experienced our first tiff. Then Richard went back to work that night, and we both started back to school the middle of the month.

    He started on his Masters and I was still working on my Bachelors. Amazingly, the very next time we saw Mother, she couldn't say enough positives about Richard. I realized that she was just scared that I wouldn't continue and complete my degree. That was something that was huge for her- to make sure that her kids got their degree. She and Daddy had never gotten theirs, and they knew how hard it was to make it without it. When she saw that I was still working on the degree, and Richard was continuing his as well, she let it be known how much she really did love him. And...when we went to pay the flower bill, it was paid in full.

35. Poor, Barefoot, but Not Pregnant

I am not saying that both of us going to college at the same time, paying rent, buying groceries, and living on $300.00 a month is easy, but we did it. We found thin plastic/paper curtains at a dollar store, made the kitchen curtains out of a set of pillowcases, made a bookcase out of cinder blocks and two 2 x 12's, bought a garage sale couch and chair for $25.00, and Mama Joyce and Daddy Coot found a stove and refrigerator they gave us as a wedding gift. I took my bed and dresser from home. We got Mother and Daddy's old kitchen table and chairs out of the storage room and cleaned them up to use. I ate baked potatoes and drank powdered lemonade mix every night for supper while watching the 700 Club and Richard ate a burger at the steakhouse where he was working. Our rent was $78.00/month for the cheapest married housing on campus in Starr Apartments #1 at SFA. Our grocery allowance was $50.00/month- that is $12.00/week. We never had to take the toilet paper from gas stations like my friend did, but we had no extravagances. One Friday night we did splurge, however. Richard was getting off work at 10PM. Baskin Robbins closed at 10 also, so I took the car, got two double dip ice cream cones, and drove a standard back up North Street holding two cones- one in each hand. I made it into the parking lot at the Red Barn to pick up Richard and parked the car. When I opened the door, one cone fell on the pavement, and when I stood up, the other one fell. I stood outside the door and just cried. We had skimped and saved for that, and now neither one of us would enjoy it! I know we didn't need it, but it just hurt that we had sacrificed for that treat, and then didn't get it after all. Every time my Daddy would come see me and eat lunch, he would always ask before he left, "Honey, is there anything you need?" It was his way of making sure we weren't going without. We made it.

The following summer Richard signed a contract to teach at Shelbyville. We found a house to rent and moved into a little green farmhouse with a two inch slope in the den floor, in the Sardis community between Center and Shelbyville. We had no paycheck from the end of May until the end of September, as you have to teach a month before you get the first check. There was a pear tree in the yard and they were getting ripe when we moved in. The landlord said we could have them so I put up every pear there was on that tree. Mother had 50 chickens that she had killed and put up for the freezer. She told us she didn't have room for them all, and asked if she could keep them at our house in a freezer Aunt Rosa Lee had given us. For rent, we could eat what we wanted. For four months we ate pears and chicken, chicken and pears, and pears and chicken again...any way and every way they could be fixed. But we made it...again. Years later it dawned on us that was another way Mother and Daddy made sure we didn't go without. They were taking care of us, maybe without the variety most would prefer, and at that time without our knowledge, but we didn't go without a single meal.

The first thing we did with Richard's very first teaching check was buy a guitar for him and a used piano for me. How about that for good sense? We actually had our first major argument over that paycheck. Since we had gone without any money for four months, we had plenty of time to contemplate what it would be like to have money and what it would be used for. I thought good planning would include furniture. We discussed it, and it met his approval. I began to window shop and located a casual floral couch, swivel rocker, and loveseat at a local furniture store that was mid-priced. I took him to look at it and again, it met his approval. When the first check arrived, I was ready to purchase. He then let me know that he had changed his mind. No warning, no discussion...just "I've changed my mind." I tried not to let him know how I felt. I went to the bathroom, began the water for my bath, and then I just yelled. Nothing bad...just getting it out. Richard was outside at the time, clueless about me being upset, burning the trash. When he heard me yell, he came running in asking what was wrong. I explained, and he would hear nothing of it. He insisted that I call the doctor because he just knew something was majorly wrong with me. He refused to be put off, so I called and when I explained the scenario to my doctor, he just laughed out loud. He asked how long we had been married, and then asked to talk to Richard on the phone. He told him that he wished his wife was like me. He had to listen to her cry and yell every month. For me to do so only once in nine months was wonderful. I will say, after Richard rethought the whole thing, we bought the furniture.

  Our first anniversary caught us in the middle of an ice storm, and we had no electricity for 2 ½ weeks. We would go to Mother's to take a shower and wash clothes. We kept our milk packed in the snow beside the well, and broke off the icicles from the roof to use as the ice in our tea. We ate our anniversary cake by candlelight, but not to make it romantic, we just had no lights. It was colder than rip, and once during that time, we woke up to what sounded like a shotgun going off in the kitchen. Richard got up, grabbed a gun, and walked the house, but we could find nothing. The next morning we discovered that the plumbing had been replaced before we moved in with PVC pipe. During the freezing weather, it had burst- all the way from the well, under the house, and into the kitchen-about 50 feet. Richard spent most of the next day lying on frozen ground replacing the plumbing under the house.

36. Time to Teach

Richard had spent the first two years after he got his degree teaching in Shelbyville. He got a job in Elkhart coaching as I was finishing up my coursework at SFA but still needing my student teaching. It still took me 4 ½ years to get that degree, but I wound up with a double major- Biology and English with my minor in Education. I only lacked one or two classes to have another minor in Math. I did my student teaching in the fall of '78 after we moved to Elkhart. I student taught in high school Biology under James O'Keefe at Palestine High School. He was a sweet, older gentleman that gave me one warning. "If two girls ever start a fight, call the office and step back. Do not try to get between them. You'll get hurt." Sure enough, about three weeks in, that is exactly what happened, but as luck would have it, he rounded the corner just as the desks were flying. It took him and about four boys to separate the two girls!!! Thank goodness that was the only event worth mentioning during the nine weeks there. When I finished student teaching, he gave me a cutting board that he had made in wood shop while I was teaching as a gift, and he and his wife came to our apartment in Elkhart for supper. What a sweet couple!

At that time, student teaching was nine weeks. On the Friday I finished in November, I left school and went to an interview for an English job at the Jr. High. While there, the principal told me of a job open in Jr. High science at Westwood, the other district in Palestine. I went Monday for that interview, their school board met on Tuesday, and the principal called that night and told me I had the job, and I observed Wednesday, Thursday, and Friday. I began work the next Monday under TC Nivens (Tomcat Nivens). I took the place of a veteran nine year science teacher that this group of kids had run off. I was really "green" and thought I would change the world. I was about to get a real education!!!

    The first week was both sides evaluating the other. I thought I could overcome any obstacle with this group. By the end of the week, they had decided the same thing about me. The beginning of the second week I told them that the previous teacher had never ordered anything to dissect for lab. So, whatever the students could bring on Friday, we would dissect. I thought this would be a rather clever way to snag their interest. Thursday I was greeted by a quart jar full of tadpoles from Ernest. I had figured out by that point that Ernest was behind, but I didn't know how much. On every paper he turned in, he spelled his name differently, so I knew something was not right. Since our class was right before lunch, and in the main building- not the lab- I asked Ernest to stop by the lab on the way to lunch and put his jar of tadpoles on my desk there so we would have them tomorrow. When the bell rang, he took off running, and when he realized he was first in line to the cafeteria, there was no way he was giving that spot up in order to deposit the tadpoles. Therefore, they went to lunch with him. The next day we got to lab and I was delighted. We had five blackbirds that Brenda, the class tomboy, had shot and brought. We also had two messes of fish that came wrapped in newspaper that two different kids had caught the afternoon preceding. I had one little fellow that kept crowding over my shoulder as I was explaining what we were going to look for in the fish, so I brought him on into the desk close by and showed him all the parts I wanted the class to see. I was so excited that the desire to learn was still inside and it just took a little encouragement to get them involved. Then I handed him a scalpel and told him to work that side of the room and I would work the other, and we would meet in the middle. He did a great job and taught the location of the different parts as well as I could have. I was so proud. Then it dawned on me about the tadpoles. I asked Ernest where they were. He said," Something's bad wrong with them tadpoles, Mrs. Hardy." "What's wrong?" "Well, something's bad wrong." "What happened, Ernest?" "Mrs. Hardy, I was first in line to the cafeteria yesterday when you told me to bring them in here, so I just took them with me, and dropped them on the porch going in the cafeteria." My thoughts immediately turned selfish. When you are 17 miles from the nearest place to eat, the last people you want to be mad at you are the people that prepare your food. "Great," I thought, "Cheryl, you will never get to eat even cafeteria food with this job." So I asked, "Ernest, did you help get it cleaned up?" "Oh no ma'am, the jar didn't break...but they all been swimming with their bellies up ever since!!" I stopped and looked at Ernest. Now I understood. He didn't know that he had killed the whole jar of tadpoles...and that explained why he brought the tadpoles to school on Thursday. He still didn't know the days of the week. Now is a good place to say, Special Education has come a long way from the days that I began teaching. I really do not remember IEP's back then, and we definitely didn't document anything other than reporting to the principal what we were doing to help the kid along. Now, ...that was the first revelation to the group of kids I had that year. Every few days I would learn something else about another one. It got to the point that when I would go home to see Mother and Daddy, Daddy would impatiently watch the clock until 9:00PM, and send Joyce and Alan to bed, pop the top on a Diet Dr. Pepper, pull out a dining room chair, and say, "Cheryl, why don't you come tell me about how things are going at school?" Most times, two hours would be gone in a blink, and I can still see Daddy wiping the tears from his eyes from laughing so hard at the events of my first year of teaching.

 Shortly after the Ernest episode, Mr. Nivens called me into his office and asked me if I was letting Calvin use the scalpel during lab. I told him with pride that he sure was- in fact, he was so good at lab that he was my assistant and would work one side of the room as I was working the other. He then shared the story of Calvin. I knew Calvin had a temper. Most Jr. High boys can have a problem with temper from time to time. Hormones are rough on boys just like they are on girls, but I wasn't ready for this story. Calvin lived with his Daddy so he went everywhere with him, including the bars on weekends. One Saturday night, Calvin witnessed his Daddy get into a fight and get knifed. He watched his Daddy die on the bar floor in front of him. I gasped. I had no idea. Then Calvin went to live with his grandparents across the road from the school. About two weeks later, Calvin was out in the pasture with his Grandfather watching him bush hog. The tractor turned over, and he watched the second male figure in his life get killed right before his eyes. I was silent. Then Mr. Nivens told me, "Mrs. Hardy, you might want to watch Calvin. On good days, I am sure he will be a great lab assistant, but if he is having a bad day, I wouldn't put a scalpel in his hand."

 I got to experience his emotional outbursts from time

to time, and his stubborn rebellion on a daily basis when it came to doing written work. In fact, his Grandmother and I had an agreement. I wouldn't send him home until he had finished his homework for me. Sometimes it was 5:00PM before he would begin. When it approached a particular time for a TV show he wanted to watch, he would get it done. I am indeed thankful that when we got to labs, we already had established a working relationship that never did falter. Calvin was always a wonderful lab assistant.

Then there was Three-In-One. That was his real name. I thought his mother had named him after the Trinity River that ran as a boundary on the back side of the playground. (In those days, teachers walked the edge of the river bank in the spring after a hard rain that flooded the river to make sure the boys didn't horseplay and push someone in; there wasn't even a fence back there.) I found out later that his mother named him this after the Holy Trinity- the Father, the Son, and the Holy Spirit. It seemed rather odd, considering what I had observed. Three-In-One was educationally lacking in motivation. He was repeating 7th grade for the third time, and wasn't passing that year either. He was huge, too. I remember him winning every event on field day for my home room single-handed!!! One day some of the boys said they didn't believe he had any drugs. Now he had to prove something. The next day Three-In-One brought marijuana to school to show them. It scared them that he actually had it at school, so they went to the office and told Mr. Nivens. The intercom came on and all teachers reported to the office immediately. He dismissed 300 kids onto the playground and all of us tried to find where supposedly he buried it. Sure enough, we found it, buried behind the band hall.

There was a Nyugen girl that was much smarter than

me. She and her parents sat up, researched, and found every wildflower, their scientific and common name, and then wanted me to verify all 100 she had collected. The students only had to have 50, and had the option of five without one name or the other, because it is not easy for 7th graders to find them all. She was the first to challenge me past the boundaries that I had established. It was intimidating to a new teacher that didn't understand at that time it was okay not to know it all.

There was Darrell. He was a tall and lanky kid. He loved science and his father was such a good encourager. Darrell had seizures. Not just space-out kind of seizures, but the grand mall seizures. I was warned that he might have one with no warning and to not bother him during it, and remove the other kids while it was going on. One day Mrs. Mullinax was passing by as I was having lunch playground duty. She said in passing, "Darrell is about to have a seizure." "How do you know?" "He is running extra hard. He will have one in a little while." I watched in amazement. It started raining in another couple of minutes, and almost simultaneously Darrell went down to the asphalt. His body began to jerk, kids began running to the building to get out of the rain, and I was there shielding Darrell with an umbrella while his body shook violently. Another teacher appeared in what seemed forever and reported that his Dad had been called and would be here shortly. Before he arrived, Darrell's seizure stopped and he drifted into a deep sleep, with me holding the umbrella over him. His Dad arrived, scooped Darrell's long and lanky body up just like he was a baby, and thanked me for watching out after his son. Later that year, we had a rare solar eclipse and Darrell's Dad took pictures of it and brought it to school as a gift for me, Darrell's science teacher. How humbling to watch a Dad be so caring for his son.

And we can't forget Brenda. What would I do without my tomboy? She was always tougher than anyone, and could beat everyone at whatever game was going on. One day during lunch while I was on lunch duty, she decided to show out. The school had a "no talking rule" in the cafeteria so she had silently gotten the entire table's attention – and not the short table- the table that runs the entire length of the cafeteria. She unscrewed the salt shaker and poured the entire shaker of salt on her pear half. Everyone (you can tell we were Jr. High because any other age wouldn't have thought it funny) laughed. As the teacher in charge, I strolled over to Brenda and whispered, "That was really cute...now eat it." The entire table left immediately and it was the stare-down between Brenda and me. She looked at me and said, "You've got to be kidding," and I replied, "I am dead serious." She did eat the pear half, and went straight to Mr. Nivens to give him her complaint. Now, I shouldn't have done that. But at the time, all I could hear was my Mother. She would have made *me* eat it. After all, one did not abuse their food. There was some poor child in China or Africa that didn't have that pear half, so the last thing you did was ruin it. (I never could figure how that would help the starving children overseas...but that was something I never got around to asking Mother. We just knew never to do what Brenda had just done, and my Mother's voice just took over my body.)

The next period got underway and I heard the intercom click on...but no voice. Mr. Nivens was good about that. He would sit and listen to your lesson from time to time, or listen to see how you were interacting with the kids, or just see if you were working. I continued my lesson and when I gave them their homework, he spoke up and told me to leave them working and come to his office. When I got there, he closed the door, something he never did, and asked me about the cafeteria. I explained the whole episode and he looked at me with a whimsical expression that I couldn't figure out. He asked, "Did you know that you could lose your job if she threw up?" "No, sir, I didn't." Silence hung in the air. Finally I asked, "Did she throw up?" "No." "Well, Mr. Nivens, I guess I still have a job then." I stood up and went back to my classroom. About a week later he called me back into his office and asked me when I was going to start on my Masters. I explained that I wasn't interested in doing that then. He told me that I had to, and began to laugh. He told me that it had been awhile since he had had a teacher with as much gump and bluff as me and that education needed some good female principals. He told me to start back to school and get my Principal's Certification. Well, he talked me into it, and I did go back to school and got all the classes taken except for the internship. At that point, we were expecting Robin and I just wanted to graduate. My classes worked for several degrees, so I got a Masters in Education- which was worth the extra $1000.00/year back then added to your contract pay. I never did go back and get the principal's certification. I was lucky to be at this school Mr. Nivens last year as principal before he retired. He will never know how often I think of him, and the influence he had on my career. Thankfully he didn't fire me when I walked out of his office after the salted pear episode. My sass could have gotten me in big trouble. Thankfully he saw a potential that I had not seen in myself, and was willing to encourage me along. I did go a different route, but did get to spend my last two years in administration after all.

37. The Big Pool and Daddy's Heart Attack

Daddy began the building of the big pool in Center at the end of my first year of teaching. (1979) He was doing as much as he could by himself and since he was pretty much a handy man of all sorts, he set fence posts, build counters, roof, etc. While roofing the swim house, he had a heart attack. He came to the house and John and Alan watched helplessly while they waited on the ambulance as Daddy literally rolled on the floor because he was hurting so badly. He was taken to Nacogdoches Medical Center where doctors confirmed that he had blown out the back side of his heart. Only a paper-thin membrane kept him from dying from that attack. He was 47. Richard and I came in and tried to help finish up the building so he could quit worrying about it getting done. It was completed, and probably not exactly like Daddy would have liked, but he ran the pool and we taught swimming there as well as in the little pool every summer from 1980 until he died in 1988.

38. Harleton Culture Shock

After two years in Westwood, and Richard working in Elkhart, Richard got a job coaching in a little community called Harleton. During the fall before we moved the following summer, Richard and I drove over to see the community. We drove up Hwy 450 from Hallsville right after a pretty intense rain. The creek flowing from Little Cypress Bottom was flooded with water about 8-10 inches over the road. We could see the bridge banisters, but that was all, and about 100 feet further, we could see the road again. He was determined to go through it, and we were driving a little Bobcat- similar to the old Pinto. Even under protest, Richard proceeded, and I began to roll down the window on my side. He asked what I was doing. My reply was that I wanted to be able to get out when we were swept away down the creek. Sure enough water began coming in under the door and the back of the car began to swerve and the tires would catch, swerve, and catch. I was scared out of my wits, but we made it through. I was a basket case by the time we got to Harleton, as I considered what we just did. Richard took me through the older side of the community by the church and we observed it was old, but clean. I could handle that. Then he took me to the other side of the community across the highway. Nice little brick homes behind the football field made me relax just a little. As we came back down the hill by the gym, I told him to let me know when we got to the town part because I really wanted to pay attention. He looked at me and said, "That was it." Tears came from everywhere. I couldn't stop. This place didn't even have a railroad, ... no hardware store, no grocery store, ...nothing!! In fact, the only thing it had was the school, a couple of churches, one convenience store/gas station, one rock building country store, a post office, a BBQ house that served two week old crock-pot BBQ, and a fire truck. Surely he wouldn't make me live here. He couldn't! But we did!

The next summer we moved to the "teacher-age." It is the house that the school owned and every coach lived there. It was a pass-through house. Within a year, or two years max, the community knows if you are going to stay or move on down the road. In a community like this, these houses can be a challenge themselves. It had hardwood floors that had turned black, green sherbet colored walls, a paneled add-on that had no insulation and sweated as bad as we did with no air conditioning, and holes behind the stove and other appliances as big as softballs. The wood rats used the holes as their highway at night. I called my Mother hoping for sympathy, and her only reply was, "You are the wife. You are called to follow your husband. If this is where he has said he will work, suck it up and buy a gallon of paint." I hated to admit sometimes that she really was a wealth of wisdom. We bought the paint, sanded the floors, and just learned to sweat with the walls. Richard even pulled out the BB gun and shot wood rats in the kitchen from the living room. The amazing part was that within two weeks we realized that God had intentionally brought us to this place. He surrounded us with a goldmine of people that would help us grow in our Christian walk, and gave us loving neighbors that would help serve as grandparents to our kids when the real ones were not here. God's plan never seems to match mine. His is always much, much better. His plan grants me what I need, not what I necessarily want. The day we moved in, as the U-haul drove up, we were met by deacons, football players, and an invite to church. They also had us completely unloaded in two hours. And yes, God used the house to humble me. It had only been two years since we left the little green farmhouse and I had grown so prideful during that time. God reminded me that "things and status" are not important to him. In fact, it hinders His work in our lives when we focus on those things. Later God gave us a nice house, but it was only after my perspective had been altered.

Richard began coaching under Coach McElroy in the fall. He had done his student teaching in Garrison under Coach Mc and wanted to work under him again. I never cease to be amazed at people. He could hunt any day with the folks from Duck Dynasty and never miss a lick. Snakes falling in the boat while night fishing was common place, but it would make his wife, Gloria, mad. He could coach a ball game until 10:30 on a Friday night and fish until dawn. He and Gloria would wash uniforms and PE socks, and walk back across the road to the house and fry the fish. I thought I was country, but how I grew up was a small bit different.

Shortly after we moved to Harleton, we learned about the water situation. There were two wells in Harleton- one on the South side of the highway that was owned by Mr. Clark. Everyone that used his well mailed him $5.00 every month. On the North side of the highway was a water well owned by Mr. Ben Newman. Everyone on that side mailed Mr. Ben $7.00 a month. No one on either side had permission to use the water for frivolous things such as washing the car or watering the yard. I had wondered about our single fire truck since we moved so I thought I would ask. "Oh yes," I was told, "we have it full so we will come out." "What if it takes more than one truck?" I asked. "Oh, it isn't to put out your fire, it is to keep the houses on either side from catching fire. Your house is a goner." Now that is reassuring!!

That wasn't the end to my culture shock... and it seemed to affect others as well. I was in a hurry one month paying bills and abbreviated our return address, which prompted a call from Gulf Gas Company. When we moved to Harleton, there weren't any available post office boxes. Therefore, our address became General Delivery, and our spot was on top of the post office boxes on the far left corner at the little post office we had. We had to collect our mail during regular post office hours, and if we wanted our mail on Saturdays, we had to knock on the closed window and tell Mrs. Busch who we were so she could bring it to the door for us. Now, once we grew accustomed to the procedure, it wasn't a problem since the post office was directly across the street from the school. When I was paying bills, I shortened the return address of General Delivery to Gen. Del. Gulf called to see if this was a prank. I didn't see how it could be since the check to pay for the credit card bill was enclosed, but I answered his questions. He just couldn't comprehend that there were not enough post office boxes available and we had to wait for someone to die to get one. The only way I got him to understand, was to relate Harleton to Petticoat Junction, the TV show. He had heard of it, and seen it. I told him I was living it.

39. Babies

I guess I began to hound Richard about having a baby after about a year of marriage. I thought it would be wonderful to graduate from college and immediately begin our family. He didn't think so, so we waited. When I graduated in December of '78, I asked Richard about our family again. He said that if something happened to him, I would have an advantage in getting a teaching job if I had a year's experience under my belt. So, I taught a year and revisited the conversation about a family. He really wasn't interested just yet. We waited still. I really wanted a baby, but I also knew if he wasn't ready, it wasn't right. I did want him to enjoy the adventures of fatherhood, and I definitely knew that it takes two on board as parents to do it God's way. When he began to come around and we began trying...we had no luck. I finally visited a doctor in Palestine and he told me that we probably wouldn't have any children. My body wasn't working the way it should.

The next year we moved to Harleton and I began to see Dr. Bianca in Longview. After several months charting temperatures, etc. he declared the same verdict. We probably would not have children. The very thing I had tried to be patient about, didn't appear to be a possibility. We continued to chart before we were allowed to visit a specialist. Two more months and when I went back, Dr. Bianca saw a rise on the charts, did a pregnancy test, and Robin was on her way!!! We were elated to say the least!! Since it was before sonograms, her sex was a surprise at birth!! Initially due on Oct. 2, we saw that date go by and continued growing. Two and a half weeks later, we had a visit on Oct. 19. I was a 2-3 then. The next morning Mother called and asked how I was feeling. She had a hunch but I was having mild Braxton-hicks contractions. She told me then that I probably didn't need to go anywhere that day and asked if I knew where Richard was. I could see him from the coach's house in Harleton coming in from the practice field, walking to the field house/gym. By lunch, the contractions had become fairly regular- with some irregular ones thrown in. Mother called again, got the update, made me call the nurse- who told me to get Richard and come on, and we went to the clinic. At that point, we were declared in labor and was a 4. By the time we got to the hospital and settled in, the nurses changed shifts at 3PM. The new nurse came in, asked how I was doing, and I explained that it was bearable, but I wanted to push the foot off the bed during a contraction. I thought it would be a good time to get some meds. She checked and was shocked to find me at a 9+. She told me not to push, and ran to call the doctor. Dr. Lucas was on call for Dr. Bianca and Robin ReShea was born at 4:12PM October 20. She was delivered without any problem- only after 3 pushes, and weighed 6 pounds, 11 oz. She was enthralled with the lights in the room, and with eyebrows furled, explored everything in the room with her eyes. She could have cared less if I snuggled her or not- she was independent from the start.

 When I went to Center for our six weeks of teaching swim lessons the following summer, I was already keying up. New or different situations always work on my nerves. Mother would watch Robin while I taught swimming- it would be a good time for her and Mother, but I didn't know how I would like being away from her all day. I also started my six weeks of swimming extremely tired. That never helps. About three weeks into swim lessons, I discovered that I was expecting again. Part of my keying up wasn't just hormones playing tricks. I was pregnant. It was a shock!! About two weeks later, I began to have problems, and a week after we got back home, I miscarried. It was a most confusing time. Obviously, we had not planned this baby, I was super busy during the time I was pregnant, and lost the baby about the time we had adjusted to the idea that maybe God had a different plan that included having our children close together rather than spread out like WE had planned. I grieved and was relieved- all wrapped up in one. It was the oddest combination of an emotional mix. We didn't name this baby. In fact, it wasn't until Dave Peterson came to our house and prayed for us and reminded us that we would get to see this baby when we got to Heaven that the reality of it all began to hit home. Later we did come back and name the baby Aaron/Erin, depending on whether it is a boy or girl when we meet him/her.

Through this experience, we knew that we wanted to go ahead with the next baby. We got permission to try again in two months...and Dustin was immediately on the way. Incredible!! I was always so fortunate as I never had morning sickness. This was the turning point with sonograms, and when they told us it was a boy, I had a shock of a different nature. We left the office and went to eat at Golden Coral. As I sat by the window, I kept thinking, "There is no way I can love a little boy as much as I love a little girl." Boy was I wrong! I didn't go into labor with him. He was due June 27th and on July 13 we induced. He arrived with the help of Dr. Bianca at 2:27 PM and weighed in at 8 pounds 5 oz. He came into the world crying, blue, wrinkled, and peeling. "Overcooked," was the consensus. As soon as they wrapped him up and placed him in my arms, he had the most searching look begging for someone to hold and love him. How could I have doubted? This baby needed me! I loved him every bit as much as Robin, but totally in a different way!

Landin came along 2 ½ years after Dustin. I was busy taking care of the older two, but this pregnancy was perfect. He was due Jan. 3, and I was neither sick nor excessively tired, but when we spent our 10th anniversary in the ER in false labor, I should have guessed that he was going to be a unique little boy. We had done the sonogram earlier, and I was tickled that he was going to be a brother for Dustin, and Dustin would be a brother for Landin. We didn't go into labor with Landin either, so we were able to decide what day we would be induced. January 9 was perfect since he would be born on his Great-grandaddy Hancock's 90th birthday. He arrived safe and sound at 3:36 PM weighing in at 7 pounds 11 oz. Landin fit right in, he really worked into whatever needed to be done, but was a very attentive baby to his surroundings.

Two years later we were pregnant again. Another little boy was on the way. We were excited to get ready for his addition. November found us half way through this pregnancy, he was moving and everything was on track. I had an appointment in a couple of weeks and found that as it led up to that date, he began to move less and less. I also felt like I was getting smaller rather than larger. Robin wanted to go with me to this appointment to hear the heartbeat. She watched with me as we zeroed in and saw the baby, but the heartbeat was silent. Dr. Bianca told me not to panic, and went to get another doctor to view with him. I knew exactly what had happened. I looked at Robin and told her, "Robin, our baby has gone to live in Heaven.

He has died." Out of the mouths of babes comes some of the most profound wisdom. She replied, "That's OK Mom. We will try again." She was right. We *would* try again. Dr. Bianca returned with Dr. Wheeler and confirmed what I already knew. Before I left that day, Dr. Bianca had to hug me and blocked the door making sure I was OK to drive home. Richard was in shock when I told him, Daddy cried over the phone, and I guess I was just numb. That was a Friday and we had to wait until Monday to verify that it was not faulty equipment. I had indeed lost the baby. Then we set up the appointment to go through labor and delivery for Wednesday. It was a long weekend!! Susan asked how she could help and I was so grateful that she came up and spent the weekend with me. We spent Saturday in the mall just walking and looking, helping me pass the time. We spent Sunday in church, I felt like everyone was staring. I felt that everyone was aware of the news, but no one would say anything. Of course, that wasn't the case- we hadn't told anyone except family. Wednesday, I was induced and the nurses avoided my room like the plague. Strangely enough, another mother across the hall was undergoing the very same thing. Losing a baby in the middle trimester is rare. Two during the same week would have been strange, but there were three of us in the Longview area during the same time that lost our babies. It was not a coincidence. Dr. Bianca said that it had to be environmentally connected. Finally one of the nurses came in and asked me why I was able to deal with this loss and the woman across the hall couldn't. I explained to her that God is good regardless of the circumstances. I didn't want to be going through labor knowing that I wouldn't get to take Dillin home, but God had already blessed us with three perfect children...and this was not the end. God wanted me to be happy because I was indeed *His* child. We had to go through this today in order to begin again. We would have to wait a little longer to complete my family, but we *would* complete it! When Dillin was born, Richard left the room. It was simply too much for him to deal with. I didn't hate him for it, and never resented him for his emotions. It served as a real reminder that it wasn't just me going through this. He was suffering just as much as I was. He lost this son, too. Then we had to decide whether to allow the lab to determine the cause of death in hopes to avoid it again in a future pregnancy, or to have a funeral. We opted for hope in the future. We discovered that whatever the environmental factors involved, Dillin's placenta pulled away slowly, and he suffocated. It was something that was not genetic, and could not be helped. We knew that we would see him once we reach Heaven, but the reality of such a loss is never easy to deal with in the here and now. Grief is real, regardless. God is the Great Comforter, but it is necessary emotionally to grieve in order to be able to move forward.

Shortly thereafter, we became pregnant with Kalin. He was an easy pregnancy as well, and again, was due 2 ½ weeks before he was induced. His due date was Dec. 4th, and we induced on Dec. 20, my Mother's birthday. We had the Hancock Christmas at our house on Dec. 3 that year and during that three weeks following, we completed the Harletone Christmas schedule and sang and played at 24 nursing homes. Each day as we loaded up, the group would pray that Kalin wouldn't come that day. I had asked the Lord myself if we could have him on Dec. 20. It appeared to be the only date open that month. I was to be in court on Dec. 19. When we got to the hospital on Dec. 20 and was hooked up to the monitor, the nurse asked if I was feeling the contractions. I wasn't. She kept watching the monitor and finally said, "You were going to have this baby today whether you were induced or not. You are already in labor." I felt really humbled that God not only heard my request, but honored that request, especially when we realize that in comparison to bringing a new life into the world, there are few things that can truthfully compete. During the day while in labor, I sent Richard to buy a new potty seat at Lowe's. Having little boys in the house causes the potty seat to take a few harsh slams along the way, breaking them on occasion. The last thing I wanted was to have company get their backside bit by a pinching toilet seat so Richard had to run that errand. The nurse came in, looked around, and immediately asked where my husband was. I told her, and she laughed and replied, "This isn't your first rodeo, is it?" Kalin arrived at 3:33PM weighing in at 8 pounds. Kalin was very laid back; anything worked with him. We got to take him home in a large red felt stocking, and he slept right through his first Christmas with his bassinet pushed up against the front door while the rest of the kids were having the time of their lives going through their stash Santa had brought.

  Although I wanted a dozen, we came to realize that raising four was all we felt that we could afford. Through the years, we have had about a dozen live at our house during our marriage. All four of my brothers and sisters have lived with us at some point, Mikey and Mersades lived with us when Joyce moved in as well. Brandee lived with us for three years, and Ana was in and out during college. Alan and Jenny lived with us on weekends for over a year along with Kayla and Kayci. It has been a full house until just recently. Thankfully, the grandkids are getting here, and our house shall be full again. Children keep a home lively and exciting, and there is a special kind of love and contentment present when a child is here.

40. Anniversaries

Richard and I spent our first anniversary dinner after Robin was born at Red Lobster. She was 2 ½ months old, we felt she was too young to be left with a sitter, she went with us, started crying, and I spent the entire meal in the bathroom trying to console her while Richard ate. Not the most romantic. Then we were "attached" again when Dustin came along. We returned to Red Lobster for that anniversary when he was 5 ½ months old- and since he was too "young" to be left with a sitter, he went with us. He began to cry and I spent the second meal in the bathroom while Richard ate the meal at the table. Oh, they still had the bright orange Formica countertops! Never again! Landin got here 6 days after our anniversary, although we did spend that year, our 10th anniversary, at Good Shepherd in false labor. He was almost a year old though when our next anniversary rolled around and quite frankly I don't remember even going out to eat for that one. I know one year in particular we didn't go out, because Robin staged the perfect anniversary dinner in our living room. She sat up the card table, set the table with complete place setting, made us go put on our church clothes, presented us with a toilet tissue roll colored tie clip and bracelet, and made Kalin sit at the bar instead of coming and climbing up in my lap. He cried and she fussed over him just like a little mother, he behaved under protest, and she had Dustin and Landin serving as waiters- complete with dishtowels hung over their arms. They refilled our tea and brought us each course of the meal. Robin cooked the meal. I remember we had received recipe cards in the mail earlier and one was a twice baked potato that was accordion-cut across and stuffed with cheese before being reheated in the oven. I do remember that as one of the items she prepared. To top it off, she had even arranged for music during the meal. I almost died! Patsy Cline in the tape deck!!! This one was one of my favorites!

There were several memorable anniversaries through the years. Actually, we spent our first eating our meal by candlelight. That was not because we were trying to be romantic- it was because we were in the middle of an ice storm and we were without electricity for a full two weeks. Number 6 and 8 were the Red Lobster disasters, our 10th was spent in false labor with Landin, our 16th was the Patsy Cline anniversary, and Richard and I spent our 36th looking down from Mt. Nebo across the Promised Land. That was something we absolutely never dreamed we would get to do! Then for number 38, we said goodbye as Robin, Zack, and Caden returned to Egypt.

41. Raise the Bar

There is nothing quite like the challenge of raising children. Richard and I had certain parenting standards through the years, and from time to time we went back to the drawing board on what our goals were and how to accomplish them. We wanted well rounded kids, but we didn't want mediocre kids- we didn't demand perfection (although Landin accused me of that)- but we wanted our kids to see things from a bigger perspective, follow Christ's guidelines in their personal standards, and do their best at whatever they pursued. That meant that Richard and I had to be intentional in what we did with them from the very beginning.

I think that began with a perspective of God and how we relate to people. We went to church whether we felt like it or not because that is how you teach a child that it is important. They went with us to the nursing homes to sing with the Harletones and the quartet because that is how you learn to minister and love strangers. We did mission trips together. Each one of the four has served with us on mission trips to staff camps in Wyoming, South Dakota, and Alaska. This teaches all of us to invest in others, to teach and mentor, and serve others.

There were guidelines on setting boundaries. We limited what we watched on TV. Three bad words and it was turned off. Even their language at home was to hold a standard. Shut-up was not to be used- hush would work just fine. If a movie was PG-13, we didn't watch it. We were so very grateful that TGIF was airing as the kids were growing up so Friday nights we had our once-a-week time of eating while we watched TV- and it was frozen pizza night at that. They were "hoodwinked" and thought it was a great treat. We added overstuffed floor pillows. With bath time completed early on Fridays, the kids sank into the pillows with a blanket, a plate of pizza, and we all just crashed. I will admit, I looked forward to the unwind just as much as they did.

We followed in Mother and Daddy's example in teaching the kids about their surroundings by traveling. We traveled then and still do now. Kalin made a 3000 mile loop across the Western United States when he was six months old in a car seat with his baby quilt in hand. Our kids have seen the Smokey Mountains, explored caves in Idaho, rafted down rivers in Colorado and Montana, ridden bikes down Pikes Peak in Colorado, slid down snow covered mountains on box tops in Yellowstone, fished, played on glaciers, ridden trains, panned for gold in Alaska. They have posed in front of Mt. Rushmore, shot rattlesnakes in West Texas, and Dustin even proposed at the waterfall at Petit Jean. Each of our children has an awareness of cultural differences throughout the regions of the United States, as well as crops grown, climate, and industry. They also gained a basic concept of distance while we were traveling. I still believe traveling teaches far more than a textbook or internet.

On the home front, schedules were put in place for order and sanity. These were adhered to and revered. Bath time during the week started at 7:30-7:45 for us to have them in the bed by 8:30. Most of the time it was uneventful. However, I do recall walking into the bathroom and Landin had a live toad sitting on top of his head. I asked him if he knew what they did when they got excited.

When he thought about it and it registered that animals that get excited either bite or poop, he immediately got it down, and washed his hair! I did hesitate to share that I had trouble with Landin as a 2-3 year old liking to strip naked before bath time. I caught him in the front yard a few times trying to catch toads without a stitch of clothing on. I know Cressie, Colleen, and Kim thought we must have lost our minds. I wonder if they thought we had too many kids to keep up with them all at times.

We always had a bedtime Bible story from the time they could sit in our laps for the reading of the shortest of stories- those condensed down into one paragraph. We then had prayer time. That could run from a one sentence prayer to thanking the Good Lord for 20 minutes for the bugs, dishtowels, rocks, doll babies, etc. We then, either read another book or made up Robin's famous "Dolly Duck" stories before the night-night drink and last trip to the bathroom. That was followed by guard duty in the hallway so Robin didn't escape and run back down the hall to the living room. Eventually, we moved up to Bible stories with more depth, and the Golden Book stories, although "Dolly Duck" really had a hard time retiring.

We tried to avoid carelessness with the people our children were around. We were particular with our kids as to whose house they got to visit and who babysat them. As parents, we made every birthday party they attended; they were never dropped off. We had two babysitters on standby but were only used occasionally. Donna (Phipps) Davis and her younger sister, Vivian, were the only teenagers to watch the kids. Both of them were loved by our bunch because they brought things to help entertain. Robin and Dustin always looked forward to Vivian bringing her horn from band and playing it for them. In actuality, she was practicing for the next contest, but the kids didn't know that. In rare cases, Joyce Ogden or Susie Townson from church kept them and of course, Mrs. Julie Fennell watched them during the Harletone programs while I was playing the piano. We just didn't use sitters much. Our kids grew up doing whatever we were doing. We moved a little slower, but they were involved in everything we were.

We expected the kids to do well in school. Yes, I did go sit through a class to see if my child was really behaving in the first grade, and yes, I stood over the same child's shoulder as he retook the test for AR reading level when he bombed it in high school on purpose. We did expect good report cards. We did expect respect for the teachers. We made many trips with band, ball, and Ag with heifers, pigs and chickens to support our kids. We coached one on how to "move a little" when they sing "country" in front of a crowd- and then we let our hearts fly with excitement when Robin and Dustin had the audience on their feet dancing during their first performance in an Ag talent show! I was thrilled when each of our four made Student of the Week, and I loved that their friends flowed effortlessly though our home for meals, gatherings, school projects, and holidays.

Our kids were taught a standard in work ethics as well. No one should hand them anything. Work for it. Never ask someone to do something you aren't doing yourself. Come with the intention of doing your job, getting along with your co-workers while you are doing it, and don't be afraid to sweat. We learned some time ago that children rise to the level of expectations we have of them. If we expect them to be lazy, use dirty language, show disrespect, they will. And if we hand them everything, they never learn the value of hard work or the satisfaction in doing it well. On the other hand, if we expect them to rise above mediocrity, and we give them the tools to do so, they will. In fact, they can exceed what they thought they could ever achieve!

    I want my children to always remember- don't settle. Strive. The best things in life rarely come with no effort. Reach for the best, and then work for it!

42. From This Point Forward

I have deliberately stopped the story at this point in life simply because I feel this upcoming section retelling the story of our kids will take a while to complete. Do know that this one job called "motherhood" has been my most rewarding calling. God knew how much I would enjoy my children, and was exceedingly generous with His placement of the children He loaned to us to raise. I have loved it!! It has been my foremost mission field in life. My children were exactly the ones God wanted us to have, and the others that have lived with us through the years hopefully look back and have warm memories from being here. I look forward to sharing this next chapter (from my perspective, of course) in the days ahead.

You have just seen glimpses from the first thirty-five years of my meandering memories. With this much being said, I want each one of you to know that God has been deliberate in the events of my lifetime, and <u>never</u> forget He is in yours as well. I can see that. He watches attentively to everything that is happening, He intervenes regularly for your good, and He deeply desires for each one of us to seek His companionship and guidance in our lives so that it ultimately brings glory to Him. This knowledge *alone* changes how we look at our life. He is the ultimate source for good parenting *and* good living. Depend on Him and you will not be disappointed. Above all, remember He is faithful...always. Yes, I am richly blessed.

Psalm 92:4 (HCSB)
For you have made me rejoice, Lord,
By what you have done;
I will shout for joy because of the works of your hands.

Made in the USA
Coppell, TX
25 September 2023